CHILDREN'S BOOK ABOUT ANGER

Self-Regulation Book for Kids, Children Books

About Anger & Frustration Management

BY

DOUGLAS WELCH

Table of Contents

Introduction

For you as guardians, the right wrath control strategies are a successful role model. You need to learn about tactics, methods and the pressures of everyday life and the information you need to share with your family.

Children with proactive wrath coping strategies are more likely to implicitly and not deliberately understand and handle frustrated emotions. You should also escape the tension that is frequently synonymous with vengeance.

Anger management by the parents is the most effective conflict management strategies for babies. By witnessing parents' outrage, children learn to show indignation. You would have to change your own actions to improve this behaviour in babies. Seek to prevent as much frustration as possible about your children.

Child wrath management strategies help your kids understand the onset of wrath. Warn them to mounting rage symptoms. Tell your kid that everybody's getting mad. One of the strongest examples is to let your children know that you are still upset. Allow your child mindful of a time of frustration and you address the issue in a constructive fashion.

You can help your child learn certain wrath control strategies. Teach them their negative emotions to calm and let go. Wrath is an assertion of yourself and a way to assert freedom even as a infant. A child's rage can cause various events, and violence often results.

Excellent conflict control strategies are the application in alternative habits. Tell your child when they can to get upset a new action to use. It is aimed at soothing your kid before the indignation gets out of hand. Any thoughts include counting, measuring, depicting the happy scene or trying to blow bubbles.

It's a nice starting point to fake bubbles because it's simple and helps your child to take long, steady respirations. Teach this as soon as your child begins to be disappointed or angry.

Self-reassuring wrath coping strategies are something you and your child should do to calm down if you are upset or trapped in depressed emotions. Feelings should be heard, acknowledged, examined and published. One of the best things that you can do to curb your child's anger is to show your child how to calm. It would be useful to know a expression such as "relaxation," "calm down" which would be replicated under tension.

Keeping papers are excellent tools for handling children's rage. It allows them the opportunity to express their indignation alone, so that no one else will see them. It takes a lot of effort to regulate your rage. Whenever your child will control its reaction to rage or try a different way to communicate its frustration instead of hurt, it can increase its capacity to control its wrath.

Naturally, as adults do, children get mad. This does not bother a teacher or parent who spends a lot of time with children. Child wrath management can be as critical as learning how to handle your own wrath efficiently, so that children become a role model for your own life.

When children spend time with adults, they don't really understand the feeling, they exhibit a lot of frustration. One way to assist children in handling and regulating their wrath is by non-aggression to express their own wrath.

Ways To Help An Angry Child

It's difficult to support a furious boy. However, given their limited size, some children seem to have an unlimited amount of color hidden within them. They are quickly disappointed. They scream. They yell. You might also be violent. Yet normally they blow up with relatively insignificant cases. It is important to reassure a child whose angry outbursts have become a issue that he or she knows how to handle his or her emotions in a safe way. That is how to deal with fury.

1. Tell about feelings to your kids.

Kids are more likely to press because they do not know or verbalize their thoughts. A kid who can't tell, "I'm angry," might be trying to convince you that he's frustrated. Or a kid who can't understand why he or she is unhappy may be mistaken in his or her opinion.

Start learning simple words like crazy, sad, joyful, and frightened for your kids. Mark the emotions for your child by saying, "You just seem upset right now." They'll learn to identify their emotions over time.

Tell them more complex terms like the angry, disillusioned, concerned and lonely ones, as your child gets a deeper grasp of their feeling and explanation.

2. Build a thermometer for Anger

Wrath thermometers are instruments which help children identify the warning signs of a rising wrath. On a sheet of paper, draw a big thermometer. Start on top of the thermometer by starting from the bottom with 0 to fill in the number up to 10. Explain that zero means 'no rage at all.' 5 means 'normal anger,' 10 means 'most frustration ever.' Talk what happens with each amount of the thermometer in your child's body. If your child is at level 0, but has an crazy look as it hits level 5, so once their rage hits level 10, you will sound like a wrath demon. Your child would say he laughs. Discuss how you feel about your body when you get upset.

You could feel your face burning up if you're level two and you could make your hands fuck when you're level seven.

It allows kids to realize the value of a break before their rage bursts at level 10 as they begin to identify their warning signs. Place your cold thermometer in an appropriate position and say, "What is your rage today?"

3. Build a strategy to assist you settle down your kids.

Teach kids what they should do when they are frustrated. Place them with more realistic techniques to deal with frustration than throw blocks when they are upset or hit their sister when they get mad.

You should head to your bed just for a couple of minutes and rest when you get upset about it.

Encourage them to draw, read a book, or do other relaxing things before they begin their jobs.

Calm down kit can also be built. A package may contain a choice color book for your child and a variety of pencils, a nice book for reading, rocks, a choice doll or a fine smelling lotion. You can say when they are angry, "Go get their kit cool," and encourage them to take responsibility for self-reassurance.

4. Teaching Strategies for Effective Conflict Control.

One of the easiest methods of calming an upset kid is to incorporate other strategies of conflict management. For one, taking deep breaths will relax the mind and body of your child when it gets upset. It may also help to go on a short stroll, count to ten or repeat a positive sentence. Provide a variety of talents, including driving ability and self-discipline. Angry children need a lot of coaching to help them exercise these talents when they get frustrated.

5. **Make sure angry outbursts do not work.**

Children often have furious blasts because it's an effective means of meeting their needs. If a child casts a tangle and his parents give him a toy to keep him calm, the tangles would be successful.

6. **Follow through with consequences if needed.**

Consistent training is required to make the child understand the violence or aggressive behaviour. When your child follows the rules, please obey the outcome. Efficient corrective methods may be time out or taking away rights. If your child gets upset when it breaks, help them fix it or get them to volunteer to collect money for repairs. Do not require them to regain their rights until the damage is remedied.

7. **Quite Abusive Media Stop.**

If your kid has offensive actions, it's not good to introduce them to violent TV shows or video games. Prevent aggression against them, then introduce them to books, sports, and illustrate that they can develop positive skills in dispute resolution.

How to Help Your Child Become a Good Friend

To most of us, partnerships are part and parcel of life. But as we all know we sometimes experience tension, pain, rage and sorrow with the fun, happiness, encouragement and affection that comes with friends.

As every other partnership, friendships work, and it is vital that we give our children the means to find good friends and to become good friends themselves.

Where to start here.

1. Start self-recognition.

The best mates are people who still believe in themselves and will not try someone to fill an inner relational vacuum. You will make them a good friend to others by focusing on your own self-worth and confidence (praising your hard work and accomplishments, constantly highlighting their positive characteristics, etc.).

2. Model good conduct in friendship.

Our children see what we do, and if you see and hear friends check in, surround yourself with supportive backers and spend time and money on your partnerships, they undoubtedly will do the same thing.

3. Concentrate on the qualities of a true mate.

All the key values of friendship are integrity, trustworthiness, sensitivity and being a good listener and they are definitely things you talk to your kid about now. Ignore these lectures at home to guarantee that they connect with the rest of the planet.

4. Talk to you about your special attributes and how to consider the unique talents of others.

Of course, friends don't have to be exactly the same, but although acknowledging each other's differences it is important to have certain parallels. She is more capable of appreciating and discovering certain attributes in others by talking to the children about their amazing sense of humor, intellect or thoughtfulness. Teach her to respect others for the different attributes she has throughout her life (i.e. "You are so fun to play and Maddie likes to dance. You should let each other learn your own favorite activities, because each of you are such good helpers")

5. Know the golden rule for them.

But for a certain cause it's a classic. Teaching the children to accept others only as they want to be handled by themselves opens a world of questions and situations about friendship. Conversely, encourage you to know whether a friend does not regard you too well as he does.

6. Explore expectations of friendship.

Some of the main things my mother told me when I was a kid was that, without wanting more, I would value my friends and what they would give. Perhaps a friend is a perfect match for dolls while others prefer games, while a different friend is a lot of fun in the forest. Our mates don't have anything to do with us, so that's sort of awesome really.

7. Seek out what's a bad guy.

It may be a good option to take the opposite role. Speak to your kid about what a poor friend might do — don't listen, don't even tell them how to play or avoid them — and you teach her not to do such things nor accept such actions.

8. Provide solutions to disputes.

Children still don't agree or get along well, and it's important to speak to your child about how to make up for an disagreement. Acceptance of accountability for our own errors, apologies and a constructive response are crucial qualities for partnerships and relationships.

Proven Techni ues To Help Your Child Get Control Of Their Anger

Most of us did not teach social skills directly. We brought them on the way, maybe by looking at the relationships of our parents with others. Yet our littleness will benefit from our experiences and learn how to convey feelings under various situations properly.

We are advised not to be upset or sad from a very young age. That just adds to thoughts of persecution. We may worry about violent actions by our children, but researchers warn us that this is the normal human reaction to frustration. We can't avoid frustration, but without hurting anyone we can learn to communicate this confidently.

Though immediate repression of rage is often required (for example to deter conflicts that lead to physical attacks) frustration may turn inward without being spoken, which may lead to emotional or even physical issues, including high blood pressure, stress, anxiety, sleep and digestive problems. It can also lead to actions that are aggressive or passive and can impair interpersonal relations.

Rage is not the issue itself, but it does lead one to make bad choices like other strong feelings. When upset, our heart and blood pressure raise and adrenaline spike.

We are physically evolving. We can also feel muscle pain and voice shifts, sometimes without realizing it.

Rage can obscure tougher feelings in some situations. The more insecure reality or impotence is harder to feel rage. Missing anger can lead to abuse. Missing rage.

We will avoid the detrimental consequences when they happen, by training our children to understand and cope with their anger. Children must learn to be self-confident, not hostile and communicate without being defensive or angry. Happily, validated techniques exist and they must be learned as any skills.

1. Use your terms. Use your language.

We should bring names to emotions while our children are young. The first step is to have a word to describe an emotion. The same thing also happens in annoyance, sadness, humiliation and indignation, but the responses are different. Although empathy is typically met with frustration, rage may be met with disgust.

It is OK to be upset, but it is not OK to act violently. Don't just tell that to them, form it. Check your own feelings; that might feel stupid, but it may encourage your child to go through the process. Occasionally, it may also make you feel less irritated and help you feel less depressed. It's Cool to make your children feel better by name.

2. In another person's case, imagine yourself.

Know that your child is special. The aspirations and perceptions of all in life are not expressed equally. Persons from different parts of the world have numerous customs and occasionally even disrespectful, can find yours foreign.

The level of emotional maturity of children of different ages and capabilities differ. Your views are not necessarily expressed by others. You can force your own beliefs upon them by getting angry at their behaviour.

3. Consider the "whys."

Ask about what is ostensibly the intent of this injurious behavior. Has a classmate intentionally humiliated your children or does she misinterpret an innocent comment? Is it that your child is angry or upset because the friend did not react while his son was waves?

4. Practice relaxation techni☐ues

While that sounds easy, soothing and angry at the same time is almost impossible. Relaxation can be experienced in many ways. In a tough situation, you can use personal details like verbs, phrases, or pictures.

Thinking a favorite song or story can be calming for younger children. You may practice other methods, such as breathing, visualization, or meditation, when your child gets older. Children should be advised to breathe from their belly button or do "elevator breathing." Advise the children to close their eyes and go to a "safe spot."

5. Use cognitive restructuring

Cognitive therapy allows people to take a new look at issues. Instead of thinking all is bad (perhaps even sing it in your head), consider all is amazing. Situations rephrased: This is not the "rest of the earth," but the "frusting case." Please attach a certain reasoning. Wrath is unreasonable occasionally.

6. Put different ways of coping with issues.

Focus on how to cope with a issue, understand that not every question has a simple approach and some problems take time to solve. Allow your child to think about it before you take action. Look out a solution to a problem. Your instructor is not "out to get you" but actually has trouble with a definition.

7. Work on communication skills.

Don't jump to conclusions. Learn to express what you want appropriately. Stop and listen to what others are saying. Learn active listening skills (mirroring ensures you are hearing others correctly) and think before speaking. Avoid the temptation to get defensive. Ask questions so you know what others are trying to say. Avoid name calling. Keep cool.

Talk about the source of the anger. In children, frustration and disappointment often bring on angry outbursts. Look for the underlying concern. The source may be a skill not mastered or a difficulty in school. There may be issues of self-esteem or problems getting along with peers. Anger and sadness can be intertwined in childhood.

Once the problem is identified, it is possible to provide help, possibly through getting help in school, explaining how things work, or guiding them through social skills.

8. Step away.

Remove your child from a difficult situation. Used properly, time outs are not punishment, but a way to remove an individual from a situation, providing time to reflect. It allows the individual time to calm down and collect him- or herself, and to regain control. It also is acceptable to put yourself in a "time out." Doing so retains some control over the situation, making one less likely to feel trapped.

Teach older children to make a conscious effort to not act – to remove themselves from the situation and take a break to cool down. Advise waiting before sending an email or text. Suggest walking away when someone antagonizes your child, creating time to think before deciding the next step.

If your child is sick, tired, or otherwise stressed, feelings of anger are more likely to erupt. If possible, don't put him or her into a difficult situation at these times. Teach older children to pay attention to these cues themselves. Those in an "emotionally-compromised state" are more likely to react in an extreme manner.

9. Foster empathy.

Encourage your child to see things from a different angle. And little kids will see that someone else is depressed or upset. Try adding a favourite character in the plot if they don't want to talk of their emotions. Ask your child questions to look at another side of the issue and to cope with the situation. How are characters going to feel and react?

Remind them and others to forgive themselves. Often only decent men go wrong. The lack of temper does not mean that you can't improve it. In fact, children have to accept that they are not punished by their acts forever.

10. Using satire.

We can't really find fun there when we are in the midst of an stressful situation. Disputes over fairly dumb things sometimes arise. Simply pointing these points will create uncertainty and lead to a solution. The use of nonsensical terms, such as Doodyhead, will bring a new conversation and forget the root of the rage.

11. Be generous with hugs and praise.

Physical contact can help defuse a challenging situation. A well-timed hug can ward off feelings of jealousy or frustration that can lead to anger. A gentle touch on an arm can help calm escalating nerves.

Remember to praise your child for their attempts, not just their achievements. Sometimes people fail, and there is much to be learned when things go wrong. Remind your kids of their strengths and what they have accomplished thus far. Pointing out your own failures can help your children see that they can move forward and try again.

12. Encourage exercise.

Exercise can be an effective way to work off negative emotions or "burn off steam." A good workout can make you realize that an annoyance is just that and nothing more. Regular physical exercise may also reduce frustration, a fre☐uent anger trigger. Exercise increases endorphins, and that feel-good feeling from regular exercise may carry over and keep a minor annoyance from growing unto something more.

13. Actually, self-reflection.

Encourage your child while upset to look in a mirror. He or she obviously won't like the photo. Wrath is not a pretty feeling. It is said that Roger Federer avoided his infamous actions by watching a video of his tantrums on the tennis court.

14. Be a model of a successful job.

Ome aware of your own fury. Studies suggest that their children's parenting feelings affect them. If you don't think that you are angry much, be aware how much you yell or otherwise express rage (perhaps you hold a newspaper), note what causes it and how you respond (throw, hit the wall, hit the steering wheel)!

While rage is a natural part of life, it is a more severe issue sometimes. For example, if a teacher suggests that a child's frustration is out of control, or that it impacts the child's life and even his or her health, then time to obtain assistance. If it is below behavioral expectations. Various behavioral and mental health conditions can aid emotional bursts. A clinical evaluation will help you evaluate your child and determine the best solution.

Steps to Help Kids Manage Their Anger

Children are not young people, but they have much of the same feelings as parents. Anger ranges from 'typical' children and children with other disorders, such as autism, anxiety or ADHD. And some children are probably more irritable than others.

Unfortunately, the way children control their rage doesn't happen easily. There are, however, other methods that we can use to control this. They are strategies that can also aid them in their later lives.

1. Competitions & emotions label.

Children must be able to understand and mark their feelings before they are able to start controlling their anger. Kids of all ages – including babies – will benefit from it. You will make various expressions for babies: sad faces, joyful faces, angry ones, etc. You may assist older children with the definition and marking of their feelings. Wow, when I told you to clean your mess, you were really annoyed. And add your signs to your body too: I will tell you that your hands are furious and your face swollen. Conversely, some children would prefer to express their feelings. Sketch their presence when they're sad, joyful or scared.

2. Remove your feelings.

Enable them to realize that feelings, whether it's anger, are all right to feel and communicate. I sometimes hear parents saying to their kids that they can stop crying or that it will bother. Ultimately, it's all right for children to get crazy. What is not all right is their unethical behavior accompanying frustration. It is not all right. It's okay to get upset but it doesn't hit your mom.

3. Challenge their negative thoughts

The easiest way to change the emotions of the children is to help them shift the mind. Until you get out of sight, attempt to think about your feelings.

Any children think big and poorly. I can't do that. I assume everyone is stupid. Tell them if that's true? You don't expect the teacher to be stupid. Then Luke begged for help yesterday with his homework, and he doesn't think you are actually dumb either.

4. Teach positive talk

Tell them to repeat meaningful thoughts in their minds while their children think badly. Hey, let's note this each time you think you're dumb: you like learning. You can do that. You're working hard in mathematics and it shows.

5. Identify the players.

Does your child have a pattern when he is angry? Is it happening with a certain child every time she plays? What if she doesn't get her way? You will provide her with techniques to try to avoid a trend until you recognise it. Any time you play with your friend, you seem to be mad. What's going to happen before you get angry?

6. Positive producement utility.

Good reinforcement is more effective than a fine. When you have found a cause, thank your children for doing issues properly. For examples, I found that when he broke your Legos, you told Johnny that you didn't like it. Good work with your expressions of peace.

7. Calming practice before the alarm goes off.

Both children will profit from learning how to know when they're upset before the warning begins and becomes a complete blast. This needs to be done. Seek calming and self-consciousness strategies if they're not disturbed. Do deep exercises in breathing. Listen to music that soothes. Find some yoga videos for girls. Make them remember how peaceful it feels and they can use their coping methods anytime they feel frustrated.

8. Teach what to do when the alarm does go off

If rage is a full-blown outburst, parents can't do anything unless they are cool. In the heat of the moment, they cannot be argued with. However, you should tell the boy, before they are calm and able to speak about what happened, that you are going to sit near them. It's also all right to let them go ahead, reboot themselves and come back later.

9. Model how to deals with arguments and emotions.

Children get to know how intense feelings their parents manage. For first, it might be crazy, but when you get frustrated, talk about how you work loudly through the emotions. I am angry right now that the car crashed because I didn't find my phone to contact the insurance firm now because I had a bad day at work. For a couple of minutes, I'm going to relax and breathe deeply. It's also all right, as long as they still can see the result, to have heated arguments or conversations with their babies. This will potentially help them understand how to cope with a problem, find a solution and start.

From young children to adults, everyone gets mad from time to time. Trying any of these techniques over time will help your kids learn how to better their management. Speak to the doctor of your child if you are already having issues. Rage, which results in attack or abuse, or frustration from zero to 60 so easily that you can't even use such techniques, are both indicators that you will want support.

Things Emotionally Strong People Don't Do

Anger is an emotion with a strong reflex drive. Even of the most seasoned adults cannot effectively control their rage. They know, however, that children too need support. There is a appropriate and inaccurate way of handling this. It begins by making them acquainted with and then first use the words.

Another crucial place to start, or just before you start, is from where the wrath comes and why they are so powerful. When you know them, you can get a lot better understanding of what is happening and how to properly handle them before you decide to take action. Listening to your kid is the perfect way to know them. The only thing that allows the kid to learn something about his social and mental health, is learning alone.

1. They're not able to make the most out of misery and drama. – The radio transmitter is your ear. It emits your emotions, directions and sounds – you may pick the channel to which you are tuned. Emotionally strong people realize this and change anger to make room for beneficial results. You will be smart enough in your footsteps. Step free from your foolishness. Concentrating on the positive, the negative will then be difficult to consider.

2. You're not wasting time apologizing for yourself. – People who are mentally healthy don't feel bad for their conditions or how other people have treated them. We take responsibility for their role in life, work to make improvements and take into account that life is not always easy or fair. At the end, joy is not a shortage of challenges, but rather a decent opportunity. And look at what you got, rather than what you missed. And it's not what the universe takes away from you; it's what you are left with.

3. You don't think you ought to be happy any more. – Emotionally positive people realize that joy is an acceptance mindset. In other words, satisfaction doesn't begin with the settlement of "this, that or the other thing." Gladness is what's going on today because you know what you've got.

4. This is not their ride like all the others that they contrast. – The thief of joy is social contrast. Don't equate your success with those of others and do your best. They're not you. They're not you. We both need time to move our distance from each other. People emotionally powerful realize, and they are living by the facts.

5. They're not envying and resenting the success of other men. – People with powerful feelings will genuinely admire and enjoy the achievements of others. If people achieve what they are trying to do, they are not envious or deceived. They know then that success is hard labour and they are willing to work hard for a chance to succeed. Real faith has no place for anger and jealousy. You have no excuse to dislike, because you think you're fine.

6. it's not what they think it is. – Heavy feelings should not consider mistakes and setbacks as excuses for giving up. Rather, they use loss to raise and strengthen. You will have to learn until you get it right. If they are trying to better their wellbeing or launch a new company, people who are emotionally stable expect no positive success. Rather, they use their talents and skill to their fullest degree and know the true progress takes time.

7. "I can't," They don't say. "You have the right to say that you can if you don't say that you can." You will and can find a way if you just want to do it. If you don't, a long list of lies can certainly be discovered. So please quit "I want." Turn your "can'ts" into "cake" and your hopes into plans. So, stop saying "I want."

8. We are not permitted to distract them from their fantasies by flickering tentations. – Don't get swayed by what you want by the tentations of today. Keep solid with feeling. Do now, so that what you intend to do later is possible.

9. They're not getting restless and they're not slowing down. – Those who wait don't have nice stuff. All who are persistent... work tirelessly for what they most desire in life come to positive results. When you know what you want, if you can see it, feel it and step towards it every day in a little way. Patient and continue to work. This is what people who are emotionally strong do.

10. They're not always making the same exact errors. – Once, you couldn't make the same mistake. As it is not a failure for the second time, it is a decision. It is a decision. Emotionally positive people take responsibility for their actions and benefit from their failures in the past. As a consequence, the same errors will not happen again and again. Alternatively, they grow and take new experiences and correct decisions.

11. They oppose no improvement. People who are emotionally strong are not seeking to stop transition. They are then invited and are able to be versatile to accept meaningful change in their lives. You know the transition is inevitable and you trust your ability to adapt. For a cause, transition arises. Throw it with it! Throw that with it! It won't be easy, but it's important.

12. The stuff they can't manage don't waste time and resources. – You're not going to hear a powerful emotional person moaning about delays and rainy days. Rather, they rely on what their lives can manage. They understand above all that their mindset is also the only thing they can control. After all, the moment you resolve to not allow uncontrollable things or individuals to manipulate emotions ends with inner harmony.

13. They don't hang on every word other people say about them. – Spiritually stable men, rather than the Peanut Gallery, listen to their own heart and instincts. Seek not to take things that others say too seriously about you. It is a product of what they think and do, not you. You can't actually change the way of treating you or what you think. You can only change the way you answer and how you pick.

14. They don't think everyone is out to get them. – Emotionally strong people agree in others to see the positive. The planet is full of decent men, as the fact is. Anyone who claims has not looked around, otherwise. Look back, then. Look back. Enjoy them. Love them. Talk with each other and smile. You end up seeing the good in yourself as you want to see the positive in others.

15. They don't care about everybody been pleased. – Emotionally stable people understand that all the time they do not satisfy everybody. You won't be afraid if necessary to say no or speak up. You are trying to be humane and honest, but you may disappoint other people if you do not live up to your unreasonable standards. In essence, it's impossible to please everyone. May you light up the bridges?

16. They don't think the beginning is too late. – Let's get away from the notion that the beginning is too late. Know, always easier than climbing the top of one you don't ... even though it means a fresh journey, it is always the bottom of the ladder you choose to scale. It's no reason to give up if other events haven't worked as you have planned or did not happen as easily as you expected. One direction or the other passes time. And note, only a single thing takes a second, a friendship, a desire, a sap of confidence, to change everything, for good, and to do everything. Do everything for ever. You will at least one day look back, and say, "I gave my best shot life." Come on, then come back. Try to demonstrate your strength of feeling.

Ways To Make Yourself Emotionally Strong & Deal With Stress More Effectively

If it affects your personal well-being, your relationships or your job, seeking ways to be emotionally stable will affect your life positively difficult through fickle circumstances. When it comes to tension, it can affect multiple people in different ways; certain people might sob any time they get upset (scorporated!). While there's not something wrong with any one of these cases, it makes you understand yourself even more efficiently by learning how to control your feelings and decide why you feel them.

"Emotional strength comes from the fact that you are both strong and reliant on yourself: it requires building up your internal capital and finding yourself confident in getting support and receiving help, learn to deal with misfortunes in life is a perfect way in building up your emotional power.

❖ Honor The Strength Of Your Past

It can be hard to be emotionally strong if you keep living in the past. You gotta throw away those thoughts and accept the fact that those struggles made you who you are today — which is a strong, beautiful person. "Many times we have bitterness from the holocaust, slavery or even family 'traditions' of abuse. We can instead, honor the struggles and our cultures in a way that is positive. Don't discount the struggle, but see how it can be a way to honor the strength in our past. If we can honor the strength of the past, we are a result of that past, so we honor ourselves and become stronger.

❖ Make Healthy Choices

Most of your emotional strength usually comes from within. That means you'll most likely feel your best if you eat healthy and treat your body with care. "Know that every time you make healthy choices, you strengthen yourself. Did you choose an apple over a candy bar; one point for resiliency! Did you take a walk and enjoy the view? Another score for resiliency. Honor each time you create health.

❖ Help Others In Need

It sounds strange to help other people when you're trying to figure things out for yourself. But when you're altruistic, you can become strong because the care you show for others can resonate and leak into caring for your own life, too. "Helping others builds empathy and empathy makes us better people, period. That builds resiliency,"

❖ Smile & Laugh More

For myself, there's no greater feeling than genuinely laughing out loud. It's a great way for someone to flood their system with happy hormones and lift their spirits when they're feeling down. Opt to watch a funny movie, or schedule more dates with people that lift you up. The more you engage in this type of lifestyle, the better you may feel. "Laughing from a pure place (not sarcasm) helps to strengthen your lungs, heart, emotions and brings people toward you rather than away; a support system filled with smiles is a wonderful way to increase resiliency.

❖ Embrace Your Adversities

Don't beat yourself up when things don't go your way. Failing is a part of life and how you choose to challenge and accept it can truly alter your perspective in a positive way. "Practice some positive psychology and begin to embrace all of your challenges and adversities as your greatest teachers and forces for change.

❖ Express Your Emotions

If you're feeling down, don't take that as a sign of weakness. Instead of sheltering your emotions, embrace them for what they are. "Whether it's shedding tears or screaming into a pillow, giving yourself the freedom express and permission to be human will make you stronger from the inside out.

❖ Look For Patterns In Your Behavior

"Do you always end up feeling like a victim? Pick emotionally unhealthy friends or lovers and therefore end up unhappy? Sabotage your successes and achievements? Think you want to be alone, then hate it?" Whether you feel like a victim when something goes wrong or you talk down to yourself when you slip up, examine these situations and figure out why you do and feel these things to fix these emotions and make yourself strong.

❖ Stop Judging Yourself

"Stop judging yourself. Lead with self-compassion and curiosity about why you have particular thoughts and feelings and why you engage in specific behaviors," Embrace your emotions for what they are and don't try to shut them out when you feel them. You don't want to engage in negative self-talk because it can make you feel worse about yourself.

❖ Take Emotional Risks

The more you put yourself out there, the stronger you may become. You want to exercise your emotions even if it makes you feel a little uncomfortable. "Take emotional risks that feel manageable to put yourself in situations that make you mildly uncomfortable but that may help you grow emotionally.

❖ Recognize Your Emotions

Don't punish yourself for having certain feelings. It's natural to feel down, angry or even jealous. When you're experiencing any negative emotions, thoughtfully examine them and figure what you want your next step to be. "Allow yourself to recognize and accept every emotion you have and then decide if you want to pursue this emotion or let it go," Researchers says about recognizing your emotions.

❖ **Talk To A Therapist**

"Going into therapy, even if it's for only a short period of time, can be a great way to work on your emotional issues and inner resilience level," Don't think that going to see a therapist is a bad thing. Vocalizing your worries to someone is a great way to figure out why you're feeling a certain way so you can build your emotional strength.

Allow your strength to come from within, whether that means you talk to a therapist or maintain a healthy lifestyle. Embrace your emotions for what they are and soon you'll become emotional strong.

Reasons Why Helping Others Will Make You Happier

It's nice to help others. And if you often have so much job and family responsibilities on the face, the attempts to make something greater than yourself or everyday obligations are particularly life-changing. It's going to even make you more comfortable.

You can give support to others simply and uncomplicatedly – it can be a volunteer initiative or a gift to someone in need, so it can be as simple as listening to a neighbor or opening an elderly screen.

You will know that doing something good and nice for someone opens up new opportunities you did not understand about your life. You will continue to have a sense of mission overall. You're going to feel yourself better.

1. As you support people, you know your inherent worth grows slowly.

If somebody says "thank you" really, it's an incredible feeling as they squeeze your hand and hug you. You feel needed. You feel required.

You see your innate self-esteem rising and improving your sense of ability. It gives you faith and love.

2. In giving everything to others, the sense of gratitude rises.

Feeling deep inside yourself that you have given someone your true time and energy, because you only wished to help, always enhances your charitable feelings. The love of sharing is one of the most unbelievable emotions that anyone will ever witness.

3. When you help other men, you will learn more stuff about yourself.

You can also learn more about yourself by tapping into the friendly hand. This increases your confidence in yourself or your self-worth by getting someone in need by just being there for them. Because you feel comfortable. You just continue to believe like life is getting better as you consider other people's needs.

4. If you come to their assistance, you reinforce your ties or relations with others.

We also want to cultivate partnerships or healthy connections or ties in our lives with others. Helping us build up the connections and also make new friends for yourself.

5. You will expand and broaden your skill range.

You may also add to your own personal life and/or to your own self-development, by assisting others to acquire knowledges or skills (for example, through volunteering). That is true if you just use the way to listen or just be there.

6. Helping others is a great way to reward you for all the positive things that happen in your life.

All of us have endured harder times at some stage in our lives when we need some kind of assistance or encouragement. Only remember how much support or encouragement many individuals have given you in the past. You should be grateful to take the opportunity to pay by vowing to help others to to support more.

Helping others offers you a range of opportunities that not only change your career, but can also help you feel blessed by career. You're probably going to be a lot better. Each day you are serving others, you will find your life more enjoyable, rewarding or enjoyable.

Ways to Help Kids Manage Frustration

Naturally, if parents are keeping up their infant babies, they want their best. We want to shield, nurture and provide them with all the possibility to live happily. Nonetheless, at the same time children must learn how to cope with disappointments and grievances.

Fortunately, from the beginning of childhood, struggles arise, such as, when babies try to get a drink and get to wait a couple of minutes for it. When children later, they have to wait for the toilet or learn to sharing a baby sibling with you. Knowing how to handle and resolve problems creates endurance – but parents may find it tough to back up and let kids deal with themselves

1. Be silent. Remain calm.

One might say "Easier said than done." But when your child is crying one might feel upset, furious or even ashamed, it's important that you model yourself to be cool. You should remember that being a good dad doesn't necessarily mean your kid is happy, and know that the age-appropriate anger of your kid will eventually pass away, so that you will still thrive.

Many kids may get irritated with their parent when they are in charge or find like frustrating themselves is a way of getting what they want. Being calm can deter this process and can make you focus more easily on what is needed.

2. Be fair and reliable.

Each child must be conscious that they may rely upon their parent to lead, help, care about, and love them. Also in moments of tension, understanding how to behave when they become angry will contribute to stability and security in the relationship, but this contributes at the same time to resentment by politely saying no. When parents uphold strong expectations and reasonable ideals for their kids and provide consistent warmth and affection, that may lead to a significant amount of good outcomes. When things go rough, staying calm will improve.

3. If there is no reasonable excuse for you to say no, why not say yes?

Special experiences and happiness will and should fill parental life. And it will be satisfying for both of you to give your children what they want and see their love and joy. Yeah, have fun and give in ... at times. It helps to establish a safe and close friendship.

You should also spend time to negotiate a solution, which is an experience not immediately gained by most young children. Therefore, if a solution is the case, spend more time debating whether you can make your child part of its goal, you can decide (instead of the broader, unrealist goal he seeks).

For instance, if you want an expensive mobile for your ten year old child and you would like to purchase a phone without internet but frequently, it might be the time to negotiate instead of just saying "yes" or "no." Otherwise, your child might reach a concession by saving the money to pay for half of a new gift.

4. Take the best time for a discussion.

You may have found that it may not be very effective to speak to your child when it is upset. Yet children still seek quick responses to get what they're asking for immediately. Asking them and quickly describing your reasoning also leads to smiles and enthusiasm for your kid if you give them what they want.

Unless, however, the expectation is not practical or one that you cannot fulfil, it can only lead to tension and greater persistence if an excited and adamant child describes it.

It can be good to note that if your feelings rise up, you don't have to respond directly to your kids. While your child gets upset, it may be best to wait until you all ⬚uietly rather than say no immediately and don't listen to your angry child.

Seek to choose a moment when your kid is happier, when you have had time to talk about giving in, not giving in, give in, when negotiate. Wait until you have time and without distractions you have found a talk spot.

5. Using strong abilities to connect.

Many children learn skills by parental coaching! So as you want to speak to your child, concentrate on being polite, being a listener attentive and compassionate and trying to be a role model for solving problems.

Such interventions can improve cooperation and understanding; but many kids still feel irritated and discouraged at the conversation. Recall that encouraging the children to learn to deal with age-appropriate disappointment always helps them to plan for the future they face later in life.

Helps Children Learn How To Become More Resilient

They prefer to idealize childhood as a stressed moment, but young adults alone do not save many infants from traumatic disabilities and traumas. The issues vary from transitioning to a new environment to insulting peers and violence at home, may be asked for children to handle. Therefore, the complexities present with development and adolescence will all be kept unconcerned.

The capabilities in endurance are the foundation of the potential to succeed amid these obstacles.

Creating resilience – the potential to respond well to stressful circumstances, pain, conflict, risks and even essential stress factors – will help our children deal with tension, anxiety and confusion. Resilient does not mean, however, that children do not experience problems or anxiety. Emotional pain is common when you have been seriously hurt or unintentionally hurt, or even when you know of the death or trauma of someone else.

We will both grow and encourage our children to grow resilience. It involves behaviour, thoughts and acts which can be learned over time. Tips to create resilience are given here.

1. Create links, make connections.

Ask your child how to make friends or feel the suffering of someone else, like empathy. Encourage your child to become a peer and make friends. Build a network of supportive families to support your child with their inevitable disappointments and hurts. Make aware that a child is not segregated at kindergarten. At school. Connectedness offers social reinforcement and increases endurance. Others will find peace in the greater authority, whether formal religion or personally, and your will may want to know about your own religious rituals.

2. Help your child by having him or her help others

Children who may feel powerless will help others. Engage the kid in age-appropriate voluntary work or ask for support with a job he or she is willing to perform. Brainstorm at school for children about how they can support other people.

3. Have a routine every day.

Keeping up with a routine will console children, especially younger children who long for their life structure. Encourage the child's own habits to build.

4. Take a rest.

While routines are valuable, it can be counterproductive and constantly worrying. Know how to concentrate on something other than what scares your boy. Know what your child is subjected to, whether it be television, the Media, or overheard conversations, and make careful that your child breaks away while they are disturbed. While the schools are responsible for success in standardized assessments, they do not produce children in scheduled periods during school days.

5. Provide self-care for your kids.

Take a positive example to remind your child how necessary it is to take time to eat well, to exercise and to relax. Make sure your child has time to love so so your child has no "down-time" to rest every minute of his or her life. Taking care of yourself and just having fun lets your child stay healthy and handle difficult periods better.

6. Switch to your goals.

Teach your child to set realistic expectations and only push one step at a time to them. Working towards the target — even though it is a modest move — and getting recognition for that, the child will rely on what he or she has done and will not help build up the strength to succeed in the face of problems. At kindergarten, large goals for younger children and older kids are split into tiny, realistic targets that identify accomplishments on the road to bigger targets.

7. Give a healthy self-awareness.

Let your kid consider how he or she has managed problems effectively in the past, and then make him recognize the courage he or she has needed to meet obstacles in the future. Help your child get confidence to address problems and make choices that are acceptable. Teach your child how to find the light and laugh at himself in general. Enable students at school to see how their individual accomplishments lead to the well-being of the whole community.

8. Keep it in mind and hold a positive outlook.

Can allow your kid to look at the problem more clearly and to maintain a long-term outlook while he is in front of very traumatic incidents. While your child may be too young for a long-term view, encourage him or her to see that the current situation lies ahead and that the future will be pleasant. A strong and hopeful outlook helps the child to see and keep going even in the hardest moments. Using history of school to prove that after tragic things life goes on.

9. Check for self-discovery opportunities.

Difficult moments are also the moments that children enjoy the most from each other. Let the child understand if everything he encounters will show him "What he is made of." Imagine learning about what each pupil has experienced from trying to cope with a tough situation in school.

10. Admit the change is part of survival.

Transition for children and teenagers will also be terrifying. Help your child know that transition is part of life and new priorities will override unattainable goals. In college, find out how things have evolved since they graduated and how the transition has affected the teachers.

Ways to make your children more resilient

With your family, what do most parents want? Glory, achievement at college, joy in your life and strong friendships would be high on their agenda. The kid needs inner energy to meet the many obstacles and pressures he / she faces competently to accomplish these objectives. They call this capacity to deal with and sound confident.

While the term resilience is usually reserved by young children who conquer tension and struggle, we think that it should be recognized for any child as a critical collection of characteristics. The strain surrounding them and their aspirations are not just children lucky enough to experience major adversities or traumas.

Robust children have good self-worth and are optimistic. You feel unique and appreciated. They also learned to develop practical goals and aspirations. We have been capable to address problems and evaluate, making mistakes, challenges and barriers more likely to be faced than prevented as stressors.

While they understand their strength and gifts, adaptive children are mindful of their shortcomings and vulnerabilities. You also developed strong leadership skills with friends and adults and can receive guidance and wellness in the right way. People focus on the facets of their life people have power over rather than those they have little to no leverage on.

Everyone has a proven golden path to the future. Every child is walking on a particular journey that is influenced by a number of influences including an inborn nature, school outcomes, a parenting style and beliefs and a larger community or culture.

Many guidebooks however provide values and acts for all roads of a infant. Some can seem to be all common sense. Nevertheless, even those who seem clear require continuous thought and contemplation so that what is truly important in our parenting behavior is not ignored. Below are approaches to help parents improve their young people's resilience.

❖ Empathy.

 In the interaction between parents, empathy ensures that parents will put themselves in their young people's shoes and see the world through their eyes. Empathy doesn't mean embracing any of your family, but attempting to understand their position and justify it. When our children do what we want them to do, actively loving, moist and sensitive, it is easier to be empathetic. It's difficult to get mad, frustrated or depressed, but it's the most important thing.

❖ Good contact and successful listening.

It's not about the way we communicate to someone that contact is. It includes listening our children consciously, respecting them and validating what they are trying to say and reacting in a manner that avoids power struggles and does not disturb them, telling them how they will behave, does not bring them down, and does not use Absolute such as ever "and never." Every parent will give first hand examples as they tell or re-injure a child repeatedly to do it or do not do it with little of a positive response on the child is part of it.

❖ Change negative scripts.

 If something we said or did doesn't work after a fair period of time, so we have to change our plan "and change our babies. This does not mean giving in to "or spoiling" babies, but showing young people that possible approaches to issues are available.

❖ Loving our children in ways that help them feel special and appreciated

The involvement of at least one person (hopefully several) who believe in the importance of a child is an important guidepost for creating resilience. These people do not have to be guardians automatically. These are people who express affection and appreciation through their relationships with a child and allow a child to feel special; someone a child can connect with and derive inspiration from.

❖ **Embracing and encouraging our children to meet reasonable goals and priorities.**

In order to achieve so, parents must understand that their child's personality is special. Accepting does not mean encouraging kids to do what they want or restricting their behaviour. However, it is easier for children to adapt to demands and restrictions when they are embraced because they encounter them in an environment of affection and care.

❖ **Helping our children excel by recognizing and improving their islands of knowledge.**

"Children achieve achievement in areas of their life which they and others find significant. Real selfworth, optimism and confidence dependent on children. The desires and abilities of each child are special and require time to grow. The children must be encouraged rather than their shortcomings. They must encourage them.

❖ **Let kids understand the failures are learning opportunities.**

Resilient children prefer to see mistakes as learning experiences, while those who are not optimistic often view mistakes as a symptom of disappointment. Parents ought to establish and measure reasonable expectations; stress that errors are not only expected but also anticipated; convey that even though errors arise, their children are welcomed and valued and act as role models for coping with errors and reversals.

❖ **Cultivating responsibility, sympathy and social consciousness by providing child care.**

Simply by making children jobs at home, we strive also to improve accountability. Nearly every young person is inspired to support others, though. Kids need chances in their community to make a meaningful difference. This encourages self-esteem and social responsibility by including them in charity activities such as hunger marches and food drives.

❖ **Show children how to solve challenges and decide.**

Resilient children identify problems, consider solutions, strive to find the right solutions and learn from the results. In order to improve this mentality of problem solving, parents will take precautions to make sure that they do not necessarily dictate to the children what to do. When children create their own action plans with parents' encouragement, their sense of responsibility and power will be enhanced.

❖ **To foster consistency and self-worth Education.**

This ensures that you are flexible, yet not rigid; so your children are willing to do so and will not endorse unreasonable demands, so they depend instead of unnecessarily punishing actions on normal and rational outcomes when appropriate, and that constructive reinforcement and motivation are always the strongest type of discipline.

Tips to Help Your Child Gain Control of His/Her Emotions

Most individuals, adults and children alike, encounter mental problems. Often parents fail to help their children express their emotions properly. This is incredibly necessary and helpful for children to devote time and effort to show children how to handle their emotions. Children can reap many advantages from the learning to regulate their emotions. Two possible advantages are: more concentration, a higher chance of contact with others and a reduced risk of acting on impulses. Below are tips to help your kid learn how to control its emotions.

1. Speak on thoughts and emotions.

Ensure that your child knows the multiple feelings he can have. Discuss what sort of facial expressions and actions can come from different emotions.

However, think about why he acts like this and displays certain habits as he demonstrates various feelings.

2. You should understand how others behave.

Your child must always be able to understand other people's thoughts and emotions. By being able to decipher others' facial expressions and body gestures, your kid can understand how people react and how to communicate with them. In addition, that will help him establish deeper and more substantive ties.

3. Identify techniques for coping.

Help your child recognize multiple coping mechanisms that he or she may use to maintain leverage. Your child should realize that people will lose control, but coping mechanisms to help them regain power will be different. It is crucial to ensure your child knows effective coping mechanisms, since each child is different and specific approaches are needed to help him/her settle down. Some strategy suggestions that your child may find helpful are to listen to music, paint / draw, to a peaceful spot, to move a comfort ball or stuffed toy, to blow bubbles, to drink a cup of cold water, etc.

4. Write Stories, publish tales.

When you have recognized the numerous causes that can lead to the lack of control and the correct management techniques for your boy, he will begin to reclaim power, calm down, and write a poem. You want to write in the narrative of the disturbing and the different behaviors and methods that your child uses to comfort him or her.

5. Grab him in control

Provide verbal reinforcement if your child retains control. You want to know that your child is respected and praised for addressing an stressful incident properly.

6. If out of control, coach him.

If your child does not use coping mechanisms for soothing and regaining energy, make sure to direct and feed him. Don't begin coaching or guidance until your child is relaxed. If you want to advise and give suggestions automatically when your child is angry and not in control, it won't benefit anybody. When relaxed, the child can think better and can rationalize what could have been a more effective way of coping with the situation.

7. The preparation makes better. The practice makes perfect.

Using role playing to help the child function in diverse circumstances of upheaval. It will help your child be able to manage potential upsets by planning and learning about various stressful scenarios that could arise. Seek to let the kid know what he or she will do in various circumstances individually before providing assistance and advice.

8. Lead for starters.

Kids know a lot from others and are quick at recognizing and imitating positive or negative actions that others have seen. Be a decent example and do as you say. We are human and frustrated, but you will seek to learn and use your communication techniques to keep control.

Reasons Why Recognising Your Emotions Is Important

The acknowledgment and control of your feelings is one of the most critical abilities. Indeed, people who can feel comfortable and relax down or change their actions are likely to do well in life, have stable relationships and handle challenges and losses.

Feelings are heavy and can even feel daunting. Both adults and children can find it difficult to handle and behave in ways that they feel very out of reach. For examples, did you ever feel so mad that you told someone you love you didn't want to say things? Then as you recovered, you knew that your feelings were getting stronger and you decided to deal with them differently?

We have always done so, but as children grow up, it becomes important to teach them how to regulate their feelings so that they are more able to deal with circumstances.

Teaching kids about their feelings and how to control them will help them to work through stressful scenarios and treat them calmer and more purposefully.

1. Understand the cause of your emotion's.

As human beings, we have feelings so that we can interact with our surroundings and appreciate what makes us feel good and what doesn't.

Our feelings are like our inner compass, which lets us figure out how we feel. This allows us then to decide whether we want to be in this position and to find out what we want and what we do not want in life.

We must be able to understand, realize what it is, and realize what it's trying to tell us when we have an feeling. For example, if a child spends time with a group of people who are sad, depressed and under threat, he/she needs to understand and acknowledge that his/her instincts tell him/her not the right position for him/her to be in.

When you will listen to your emotions and respond to them, you are more inclined to gravitate to someone who can make you feel good about you. A kid who does not realize that his / her preferred community of friendships has a negative effect on his or her well-being.

2. To make you feel guided more.

Our mood and actions will profoundly influence our emotions. It can affect friendships, family relations, schoolwork and our overall feelings of satisfaction if you feel upset, nervous or worried.

Being poor can also make kids feel like they don't want to engage in sports or events outside the classroom. We can help children understand why they are sad, so they can understand why and seek to find a solution that will make them feel better. Getting the opportunity to care about your emotions and to know you will make a big difference to your purpose and control over your future.

3. Negative emotions can lead to negative thoughts

This can lead to negative thinking if we struggle to remember it when we feel unhappy.

It is very important for parents to make kids realize that they are responsible for their feelings. When you spend a lot of time thinking stuff like, "I aren't good enough," or, "Nobody loves me," so that can influence your attitude and the way you view scenarios.

To show children that they are capable of improving certain views and of determining what they think will alter attitudes and inspire them to young people who are willing to reframe cynicism, be happy and trust in themselves.

The lesson that children will learn is that they can do things, because they feel that they can. They just have to believe that. The first step towards positive mental health and well-being is when we feel depressed and change critical thinking.

4. This means that we can seek assistance.

Often we need support from the people around us-friends, teachers, or a friend while we feel down.

It is necessary, because sometimes children cannot understand that they need support with their emotions alone. You need constant feedback and mental encouragement to help you learn how to relax.

Sometimes children only need a cuddle because they are overwhelmed by their emotions by someone they trust. For someone, without prejudice, to listen to them, concentrating on their thoughts, not their case. Children must realize that they can share their major emotions with a trusted person who can lead them.

A way for children to learn safe ways of controlling their feelings is to enable them to connect with and understand what they need to support them.

5. it's helps you be a good friend.

You may teach you to understand their own feelings, control them and express them to others. Children who understand the emotions of individuals very well would be able to see whether their environments are not really comfortable and will respond accordingly and support them. When they grow up, they can help their family, peers and others around them to build stronger relationships.

Proven Ways to Encourage Your Kids Effectively

Young children must be inspired and supported so that in their life they have clear goals. If used correctly, words of affirmation will have a very positive effect on the life of the child.

Words of affirmation in the right manner, whether at school or at home, will support children in their growth. Children are looking forward to what they do. Although they are scolded for being unheard of and breaking things, when they do positive things they should be praised.

It is very normal for children to try new things as they grow up. Both parents and teachers should be conscious of what they do, and should be motivated to find opportunities to do.

In your life you never know what terms children bring with you. And, when it comes to inspiring them, you must pick your words carefully. Words which are no practice but words instill ideas which will endure for a lifetime into the minds of children. Here are the demonstrated ways to effectively inspire your children.

1. Story Filled history.

To make a world full of stories for your kid is one way of making your world exciting. Take a book and read it to them. Take it with you if you are of the age to begin reading it. Enable them to read and hear the tale aloud. This graves in their heads the words in the story and helps them to connect more later on.

2. Sincere appreciation and honesty.

You have to sincerely and genuinely compliment them. Insincere louanges can be dangerous not only but counterproductive. It is futility to assume that an genuine and deceptive motivation will not be differentiated. They appear to say 'I wasn't good enough because I remember' unless they get a perfect recognition. These praise will lead to autocritical childhoods and must at all times be avoided.

3. Specific and detailed Comments.

Relevant and concise comments can be used instead of generic comments. It is best if you are a genius to answer the issue 'I love that you are able to come up with a reasonable solution to the dilemma.' These concise remarks are interpreted by children as accurate and genuine, and less general commentary.

4. Praise not their capacity for their efforts.

Children may make a distinction between loudness and ability. It is widely acknowledged that we are appreciative of the effort they have made to solve a problem. Effort should be used as a long-lasting goal because children seek to enhance their actions rather than claim that regardless of their abilities they are able to do it. Children may assign performance rather than ability to their actions.

5. Avoid Controlling or Conditional Praise

In order to monitor or exploit attention, constructive knowledge would be preferred to contolling. In childhood you are conditionally allowed to give your childhood a dependent self-worth. You ought to make sure the affirmation is not used as a coercion device. Self-worth is nothing more than what they consider more people deserve. Also note also that recognition is not to dominate but to encourage your children.

6. Do not equate.

You may be likely to equate your kid to others. No, it cannot be believed. Parents and teachers prefer to equate them with other children in school, sport or parenthood.

It also makes kids inspire themselves to see another kid do. Yet it's going to get harder if it back fires. Your child may feel insecure about not being good enough.

Only assume that you are contrasting your good colleague. You are inspired and enthusiastic if you do well. But if you crash, you will feel less inspired than discouraged.

7. Unnecessary praise.

Many parents overly applaud their children. This impacts children adversely. When kids are applauded for straightforward activities, they prefer to lie down and do not try hard things.

Children who are rewarded for easy things will only do what their parents want and do not carry out difficult activities. They prefer to do things in a way that makes them enjoy more than play with new things.

8. Hands on experiences

Let them do basic things themselves in everyday life, be there next to them, but let them do them. Washing dishes, planting saplings and getting your dog out for a stroll are just some of the quick things you can do on your phone. This fosters a sense of everyday life and related issues. Your kid should appreciate the routine requires, and the better if he / she's happy to do it.

9. Big time for practice.

All works and no play make jack a dumb kid. Give them plenty of time to play. When they are young children will and will have a great time. They always see the need for a rest during their research in this manner.

10. Motivation and compensation.

When your children do what they deserve, it is necessary to offer incentive and encouragement. They also replicate it and make it their routine if they are given a compliment when they do something good. A healthy practice when reinforced is a habit and lasts all their lives.

No matter what the age of your children is, whether you teach them right and wrong early in their childhood.

Children gaze to their parents and see how they live on earth. Curious and imaginative in this generation, children have a fast learning curve, unlike adults who have a slower learning curve.

Children should take whatever is learned at this age with them their whole lives. The only thing that parents can do for their children is purchase a ton of toys to keep them in place. We need plenty of space to make use of and develop their imagination.

Ways to Teach Your Child Anger Management Skills

If your child does not know how to control his feelings, resentment and rage will quickly become rebellion, contempt, hostility, and tangles. When left out of control, adolescent violence, including fighting, swearing and bullying, has been related to school issues, peer refusals and adult mental illness. These five techniques will teach her anger management skills, if your child has difficulty reducing her temper:

1. Distinguish between emotions and actions.

Wrath is an common feeling that is stable. But many children have trouble knowing the distinction between rage and violent behavior. Prepare to mark your child's emotions so that it can speak out about feelings of resentment, disappointment and deceit.

Say, "It's good to get upset but it's wrong to strike." Encourage him to understand even when he gets frustrated he is in control of his behavior. Aggressive behavior is often the product of a multitude of discommodity emotions, such as depression or humiliation.

Chat regularly and over time about feelings and your child can become more aware of your feelings.

2. Model Appropriate Anger Management Skills

The easiest way to teach your child how to cope is to show him how he or she deals with feelings when he or she is upset. He would also also do the same if your child sees you losing your patience. But he will pick up on that as soon as he sees you coping with your emotions in a more children's way.

While shielding your child from the many issues of adults is vital, it is safe to teach him how you treat angry feelings. Present moments where you are upset so that your child knows that sometimes adults are too crazy.

It's all right to say, "I'm mad, because I didn't stop the car in front of us to let the kids cross the lane. The thoughts will also encourage the children to think about his emotions by verbalizing them. But, I will wait to cross safely.

Take control of your actions if you lose your coolness around your babies. Excuse me and analyze then what you need to have done. Say, "I'm sorry today when I was nuts, you had to see me screaming. Rather of raising my voice I would have been on a path to calm down when I was frustrated."

3. Set up Anger rules

Many households have implicit informal guidelines on what behavior is permissible and what is not permissible in response to frustration. Some communities don't know about closing doors and lifting voices while others are less accepting of such behaviour. Develop written guidelines to explain your goals.

4. Study safe skills for coping.

Children need to learn how to deal with their rage. Rather than saying, "Don't touch your dad," explain what she should do if she's upset. You can also say "What can you do other than hit?" to help your child continue to recognize techniques it considers helpful. You may also suggest, "Take your mouth and walk away from your child while you are upset." If she's angry, you can build the friendly package she will use.

Fill a box with things, for instance the coloring book and pencils, the scent of good lotion, or calming music. The presence of her senses will allow her and her body to calm down.

To help your child rest, use time-out as a tool. Teach her so she should spend time with herself when she gets into trouble. Having a few minutes to get away from the situation will allow her to relax. Provide problem solving strategies so that your child can understand the challenges should be overcome without violence. Discuss options to effectively settle the dispute.

5. Provide results as needed.

When he meets the laws of frustration and adverse repercussions when he fails the laws, show your kid positive consequences. A child may use its anger control skills when it's angry because it has a good effect, such as a incentive program or a token economy program.

When your child is violent, follow up with immediate consequences. Time-outs, lack of rights or compensation may also be caused by taking out additional tasks or renting a gift to the abuser. Children often have trouble controlling their frustration. But the abilities of your child should strengthen with your guidance.

If your child is unable to manage his rage, or his symptoms with frustration begin to escalate, seek medical assistance. Skilled clinicians should exclude any potential issues with mental wellbeing and assist with the growth of a behaviour.

Reasons Why Expressing Your Anger Immediately Is Magic

At the time, you're doing nothing. You're tented and talk about what's happening. Wait before you find a good way to express your feelings. Perhaps think about it while the children sleep. Or maybe you prefer not to say anything. More critical matters are to be concerned about. The boat will not be shaken. Or forbid Heaven, fight. You're not in pain.

You don't even know often when you feel depressed or upset. You missed the catalyst a couple of hours later, and you wonder why you're in bad mood. Say it, please. As long as the feeling occurs. It is so important that I advise you that when you see the smoke, you have to bring a fire out. Will not wait until it's a trap.

❖ **Normally, they are less powerful than you would have expected.**

It's because we sometimes think about things that magnify our feelings. You won't get to come up on additional ideas until you get the idea out fast. It is easier to work with a more controlled feeling. A lot of people claim to wait, because you're not going to do anything you can regret later, when you feel frustrated. You just have to say why you are upset with the other guy. Why are you going to regret that? No positive or negative emotions.

❖ **The other side Understand better**

You don't waste time debating about who did something when you express an feeling related to something that just happened. There, in front of you, is the case. You can't work up rage or grief and blow up with a minor accident. The receiving group gets puzzled as we erupt with repressed emotions. Where did all the feeling come from? That is where confrontation usually occurs.

❖ You gives the other party the opportunity to clear up their mistake.

I found it's because of a misunderstanding half time that I got upset with my husband. I missed what he meant. I offered him the chance to clarify by expressing the sentiment rather than dismissing it.

❖ It is impossible to be resolved if you do nothing.

Your wife or children cannot allow you to read your mind. They can't guess you're mad if you don't tell them how you felt. If they help to fix the problem, you may be shocked.

❖ You do not have to 'fake it"

It is exhausting to think and feel one way and act another. You are important for your mental and emotional wellbeing to be genuine and congruent.

❖ You don't store emotions.in your body

Unbelieving feelings doesn't cause them to vanish. Almost the reverse. Repressed feelings are related to a wide spectrum of symptoms. Increased risk of diabetes, hypertension, infectious disease, anxiety and depression included.

❖ Your feelings would be your friends.

Many people don't believe they should feel bad. It's a disruptive power to be scared. You make them your friends by acknowledging and sharing bad feelings. You will provide useful knowledge to help you decide. And when you're off line, they'll announce it.

❖ You continue to feel the other way around.

You would think you wouldn't be sad, upset, or scared. Your aim is to resolve those emotions. Why do you focus on or give you room for air? Oh, this is its charm. The only way to let them go is to acknowledge and convey the bad emotions. Mind that after you talk to a friend, how comfortable do you feel?

❖ **You create intimacy**

Some people don't express feelings because they risk rejection. But only by being honest, open and truthful can you create good relationships.

❖ **It would be the same for your loved ones.**

By expressing your emotions, if you set an precedent, your loved ones would be much happier to follow suit. They are getting the same advantages by doing so. They are physically safer. Your friendship is going to be improved. Start with the ⬜uestion: What do you feel? What do you feel? '

Tips To Help Your Child With Anger

A kid – like anyone else – gets mad. We shift into battle, flight or freeze when we feel threatened. Wrath is the reaction of the body to 'war.' However, people are not only upset in the face of external challenges. If today it is reminiscent of a past upheaval, we are annoyed about defending ourselves-even the today's threat is not so much a danger. That is why we cause our indignation through our three year old defiance.

We are still upset about failing to keep our balance. And if we're too distressing in our anxiety, harm, deceit, pain or sorrow, we prefer to clic. The wrath does not break free from the damage, but it makes us feel less helpless and stuns pain. That is why coldness is part of the complaint process. And citizens mobilize by attacks against any perceived danger (including our own disturbed feelings).

This also extends, of course, to girls. And because the children have no background for their upsets, the end of the planet may sound like a little frustration. Worse still, infants are much more vulnerable to astonishment because they don't have a completely formed frontal cortex that allows them to self-regulate. Often hitting makes sense when we are upset, but only when there is really a threat.

(Isn't it insane to think that we can use the anger constructively when we adults do?) This is rare. Most of the time, children get angry and they begin to target their younger brother (who has broken their genuinely precious memorandum), their parents (who have disciplinated them "unfairly,") their teachers (who made them embarrassened) or the bully on the playground (who scared them).

Naturally, children need to know these skills for years of parental instruction. In the graduate school years, if parents can make their children feel comfortable enough to communicate their frustration and to discuss the feeling below, children can push past their cold into positive problem-solving. Here are tips on how to give your kid good wrath management in everyday life.

1. Begin with yourself

If you are used to screaming at your children, know that you model your child's actions. You can't stop yelling at your child, but you can't trust your child to learn to control him / her if you give in to the urge. Your child must know how to deal with conflicts and disagreements.

And when he's upset, your soothing presence allows your kid to feel safe, helping him build the nerve pathways in the brain that avoid the battle and flight reaction. That is how children learn to relax. From the self-regulation, it is not so scary to know where rage and other distressing emotions are – moms and dads don't hate them, after all.

2. Deescalate.

When things go right, you're usually happy to keep cool. Heroic actions are required to stay calm as events become chaotic. However, yelling an agitated infant reinforces what it always knows: that it is at risk. (If she just socked her little brother, you might not know how she would believe she was at risk because the kid who attacks is a kid that feels threatened and defensive.) Yeah, it's just the rage that would make the storm worse. Your research is peaceful again and only when children are relaxed are able to think and understand how to "be better."

3. Note that all emotions are permissible.

Your child must know how angry he is and that you get it. So, listening and remembering is the right thing to do when he demonstrates frustration. Obviously, you don't have to admit that he is angry and has a right to be. So don't tell your child to relax or to behave appropriately at the moment. This just increases your child to get you to understand. Instead, just open the contact door: "You must get so messed up to talk with me like that. Tell me all about it."

No, you don't encourage harassment. Please note, any emotion is appropriate and only steps must be restricted. Such thoughts are no longer under rational control when you ask kids to 'cover' their emotions. And they'll come out unchecked and your kid will definitely have a short fuse. The child will embrace the feelings instead of attempting to control them if feelings are allowed. This gives her some conscious power over the stimuli so she can start expressing them in sentences rather than touching them.

4. Give your child ways to manage his angry impulses in the moment.

Children need to be capable of coping with their frustration right now. If your child is quiet, list effective strategies for coping with feelings, follow them, and put the list in the fridge. Let her compose, or add her pictures, so that she can feel like she owns the list.

One comment regarding the actual expression of anger. Note that the treatment does not conduct the violence, which ultimately will make the individual angrier. But that will happen by dancing, the body can take advantage of the loading stress. What encourages your kid also is that he will show you how upset he is, and he is accepting. And if your child tries to hide something (instead of acting on someone's anger), say "you show me how angry you are! I see! Yeah!"

5. **Help your child be aware of her "warning signs.**

As long as children are in complete flush of dopamine and the other neurotransmitters "run or flight," they realize it is an emergency and are battling for their life. Allow them to learn the "warning signs." At this point it is almost difficult to deal with the violent urges, because what we can give children is a safe haven as the hurricane fills them. But if you can make your kid realize when she gets irritated and tries to cool down, she will be even less in tanning. When she is young, she may need to learn about her signs and take protective steps — to get some time to snuggle to keep her out of the food shop.

6. **Set violent boundaries.**

Accepting emotions does not mean allowing destructive acts. Children, and their parents, will never be allowed to harm anyone. They always ask us to set boundaries and help them control their wrath. SAY "You may get just as angry as you want to but I won't let you harm me. I'm trying to keep both of us in safety. You may tell me why you're angry without hitting me." It's safe to let them combat your hands or even your body, if you want to, just keep your glasses away and don't let yourself get hurt.

Likewise, don't let children in their fury smash things. That further adds to their culpability and their feeling of being a poor guy. Your job is to be a secure container and a testimony when you are experiencing the upsets of your kid.

7. **Don't Send a child away to calm down herselfs**

Your goal is to maintain a sense of health, which involves your calm presence, when your child is angry or upset. Notice that children are in need of your love if they "earn least," rather than "hour off" which gives children the impression that all of them have this wonderful, terrifying feeling alone, just seek a "time in." When you follow this approach, you would be shocked by how your child starts displaying more control as he feels less powerless and lonely.

8. Restore links

Your child must know that you understand and support. When you know what is going on, confess it: 'you are so upset that your tower is falling.' If you don't know, explain what you are saying; 'You weep very much... I can understand how mad you are.' Give clear permission: 'Everyone has to cri (or gets frustrated, or feels very sad) at times.

9. Do precautionary maintenance to help your child work through everyday emotions.

There are a variety of activities that make the child mindful of the social difficulties that all children face in their everyday life. They support her perform.

10. Help your child develop a sense of emotion.

Children who happily treat their cold constructively with their emotions. Unfortunately, some kids don't feel comfortable when they show their frustration. Even parents find their worries and disappointments ignored or even mocked. Often they were sent to "rest" in their rooms and never were helped to deal with their agony. Often it's either too traumatic or grievous.

They try hard to repress anxiety, envy and anxieties, but repressed emotions are like a pre-school baby enters unexpectedly, without control. Such children are fearful of their emotions. Those children get mad, so they remain mad to fend off the pool of terror, sorrow or other suffering. A child will benefit from medical care if this occurs.

When a kid gets "people with anxieties" it means that he hates the emotions pent-up (fear, pain, sorrow) that he feels will ruin him and he hardens his heart in anticipation of the vengeance that he believes is going to consume him. Children grow a chip on the back of them. You feel like they are trying to push you running, but it's a plea for assistance.

Start by including your child's ideas in this book. Start learning about feelings in your household. Don't wait to receive medical assistance if you don't find that things are improving after a few months' hard work. An skilled therapist may support the child to handle these deeper emotions and to learn more emotional handling. In general, though, I propose that parents go with their child to counsel. You don't want your kid to believe he's broken and you're forcing him to "fix" him. You want everyone in the family to learn how to connect properly. You can be supported by a good therapist who can support you and your kids.

Signs You're Raising An Angry Child

Often everyone gets mad. And wrath is a natural, wholesome emotion. Nonetheless, some children are almost still mad. Children who are upset fail to survive. You get into fights while playing games, complain when you do something fun and you can't bear being told no. Several things can make a child upset and violent. The issue may arise from unresolved feelings, such as sadness in connection with a breakup or death of a loved one. A history of abuse may also contribute to intense frustration. Problems in mental wellbeing are also associated with episodes in rage. Children with depression, anxiety, illness in opposition or hyperactivity in attention deficits fail to control the thoughts of the infant.

Some children seem short-fused to be born. If they aren't pleased, they are restless, intolerant and genuinely hostile. An seemingly insignificant incident could lead a angry child to a complete meltdown within a matter of seconds. The entire family can be exhausting in coping with such aggressive and erratic behavior.

Although it can be appropriate for young children to throw tongues and pre-school children at times to scrutinize violently, it is always necessary to keep an eye on action that goes above and above usual childhood behaviour.

Here are few early signs showing that an angry kid may be looking for medical help:

❖ **Outbursts of anger mess with relations.**

It is common for young children to strike a sibling or call someone a name once and for all. If the angry outbursts of your child prevent him from sustaining friendships or the willingness of your child to establish sound ties with family members impacts his actions, however, address it as early as possible. Otherwise, long-term partnerships can be a persistent challenge.

❖ **Your Child's Behavior Disrupts Family Life**

Even your own house, you shouldn't step on eggshells. It is not safe for everyone in your family if your everyday lives are interrupted by the wrath of your infant. Temporary fixes that contribute to longer lasting issues are slipping over your child or handing them in order to prevent a crash. The animosity of your child may escalate.

Worse still, certain members of the family may become resentful. If you lose fun or if your time with another child is disrupted one by one, then the action of your unhappy child is a issue that needs to be overcome.

❖ **Aggression is a weapon for your kids.**

Aggression is meant to be a last resort. However, caught-out also is a first line of defence, for children with rage issues. If your child has difficulty in solving issues, resolving disputes or asking for assistance, he will use provocation to resolve his or her needs. Teaching different skills will also encourage a child to understand the violent behaviors.

❖ **Temper Tantrums Aren't Age-Appropriate.**

But for a 2-year-old, it's natural to throw yourself down to the floor and stomp your feet in a crazy state, for an 8-year-old, that's not usual. Meltdowns will decline as the child matures in frequency and severity.

If the mood of your child seems bad, it's a sign that you have trouble controlling your feelings. He definitely needs to be taught and trained to help him express his emotions with maturity.

5. **Your child has poor anger resistance.**

When children mature, they should be able to handle stressful behaviors more effectively. If your 7-year-old throws his construction toys as his inventions tip over, or if your 9-year-old crumples his papers any time he errs with his homework, it may be important to help develop a resistance of disappointment.

If you have trouble making an upset child feel better, consider seeking medical assistance. A practitioner in mental health will help you teach techniques to manage your child's frustration. Any psychological concerns the child can should be discussed by a psychiatrist.

Starting thinking about your issues with your child's pediatrician. Your child's health care professional will request a referral to a mental health specialist if necessary and would try to exclude any medical conditions that may lead to the question.

Ways to Help Misbehaving Kids

Poor behaviour is often a symptom of worrying kids — and the only remedy is retribution. This idea about the value of self-control influenced the way we thought of actions and that of our children. "It is the first and noblest of all victories for the human to overcome itself." If they had only strong willpower and spirit, they could well and avoid tentation, will they?

The aim of the self-regulation is to recognise our stress ors, the their severity, find quiets and learn ways to relax and rehabilitate.

To learn how to help our children is important to learn the difference between self-regulation and self-control.

Growing child will be directed along a journey leading to a rich and fulfilling life through experiencing empathy and caution. Yet the "poor child"'s assumptions so often shade, even as we as parents hide from our hopes, worries and fears. When we view children negatively, we are unfairly passing the blame back to the 'culture' of our children regarding our own feelings and fear, instead of trying to consider the psychology of tension. Recent advances in psychology open up the mysteries as to why we are behaving the things we are and why it's really impossible to do how we want to. The limbic system plays an important part here as it gives rise to our intense impulses and desires, as well as the crucial role that we play in the development of our memories and our emotional experiences. This program helps us respond to threats and complaints, but it is completely out of our influence, even child protection.

Children with heightened emotional activity may have very reactive limbic structures in which their brains are programmed to respond to threats, even though they do not appear. Experiments have, for example, shown that children who are excessively over-rushed are called aggressive neutral ears.

This suggests that children who respond with aggression or shut down usually show the outward symptoms of an internal stress overload encounter. When we don't understand the symptoms to find out what is troubling them, we must help them deal with them rather than better or bad, rather than with guilt, warnings or retribution.

The reaction of a parent in the early life to the stress of a child is essential to his capacity to self-regulate later. The aim of Nature is to improve the role of human parents and to take advantage of the "interbrain" – the innate contact mechanism between the parents and the children that maintains a mutual feeling, a mutual look and expression. That aids a depressed child to learn a way to calm and deal with stressors in their lives. This allows them

The availability of moist, early-life treatment will go a lot to handling stress. This does not mean, however, that parents alone are responsible for adjusting to their infant. Self-regulation can also be troublesome for children who have encountered moist and caring parents. That's why knowing how it works is critical and how we parents can assist.

Here is the strategies that will allow parents to cope more easily with their children's issues or anxieties:

1. Recognize that the kids' pain is over.

Part of your job as a teacher requires learning how to understand the nature behind behaviors, which can be confusing or frustrating otherwise. You are free to fail to assign blame or names to your children as you learn to read the signals and understand them as what they are — a symbol of a device overcharged. The first and potentially significant step towards self-regulation is to refram the actions of your kids as a response to discomfort rather than intentional misbehavior and learn to listen to and observe your children with curiosity.

2. In the children's lives, recognise stressors.

Stress in kids also entails frustration in marriages, schoolwork and other intentional tasks or too little time to do. But even pain and biological origins may be covered. Any of your children, for instance, become extremely disturbed by too much noise, light or scent and this can create persistent, unseen difficulties in your life. They also can be highly frustrating with their isolation, waiting or sitting. It is important to look at all these stressors from a number of sources — biological, physiological, cognitive and social fields.

While our world can be incredibly overwhelming for our children, we sometimes ignore evidence to warn us about this. We — or they — might start as though it weren't relevant.

That does not mean that the unconscious mind does not monitor tension and react with tension, though, which can trigger a challenge, flight or freeze reaction.

Families should look for behaviour patterns — like the children who often split up at 5:30 p.m. . . . — to make them understand the stressors of their children — maybe they hunger at that time. Or, if less straightforward, try to test the various aspects of your life in your brain and what could cause tension. No matter what you do, do not respond in anger or judgement to further exhaust you. Start listening then to asking the kids calmly what's going on.

3. Minimize stressors.

It is amazing how simple stress relief can easily transform the behaviour of a child. Only after she noticed that the light in the classroom had dimming dramatically altered her conduct, I found the girl prone to noise, light and textures identified as a "poor child" by her teacher. Sadly, the child's decision had been accepted for some time before, conveyed through raised voices and distorted facial expressions. Currently, her father and grandparents were branded complicated as well.

The same will happen to parents who don't pay attention to the pressures and sensitivity of their children. Once causes of tension are established, either by pushing our dinner hour back, by dimming the lights or by giving them a hug after a missed exam, it's much better for the children to stop or to reduce them the best we can.

Often it includes understanding what we are thinking and how it impacts our actions to minimize our children's tension. Learning to relieve our own tension will help us control our feelings and make our children less emotional when they fail and provide them with an significant role model.

4. Help the kids find calming techniques for them.

Both of us need conflict management techniques and energy recovery. It is important to read signs in your children, to understand their particular sources of stress and to ensure that their self-regulation methods match their needs. No one size fits all.

Care was marketed as a means of instilling relaxed energies and raising consciousness among our youngsters. Yet our children often may become used to extreme tension, which means a hypersensibility is "natural," so much so that they can be a thousand times more distressful than they are anxious while simply sitting and concentrating on their breathing – a traditional conscious activity.

It can be incredibly rewarding to encourage your children to develop slow sensitivity and strategies for calming to encourage them settle down. Teaching the children mindful breathing – if performed gently and with guidance – may be one strategy that allows them to become more aware of their relaxed needs.

But it is critical that your children do have calming strategies as fun and that they do not unintentionally contribute to their tension. Many calming activities are available to offer calmness, such as yoga, a stroll or focus on art projects. Encourage the children to check what affects them best and help them find relaxation.

5. Take a long-term look.

Of starters, a child can be silent while playing video games, but neither of you can confuse it of calm so you shouldn't. If you should help your kids with yourself-regulating techniques, understand the difference between "still" so "calm." If they play video games in a relaxed and distracted environment, their brain releases stress hormones. The point of seeking solutions is not to promote your life in the short run (by keeping your children still), but instead to make your life more comfortable and successful in the long term (helping them to cope with tension in a balanced way). Naturally, taking my advice does not mean that your children are never mistaken or that any of their problem behaviour.

Yet many misconducts are a call for help — a call we must respond with compassion and empathy as parents and as adults rather than with retribution. It does not ensure your child can instantly avoid you annoying or upsetting after the steps of self-regulation, however, it will help prevent needless distress. Our research revealed how children are able to improve their behaviour by taking these steps. When your kids know that you truly appreciate them and dedicate yourself to doing what you can to improve, your relationship with them and the ability to deal with the struggles of the life can be strengthened.

Positive Ways to Help Kids Manage Disappointment

You, as a mom, never want your child to suffer. There may be both physical and mental pain – all of which are also difficult. Disappointment is one of the worst things for a boy. Kids may look forward to activities, activities or milestones. They can also encounter deep feelings of disappointment as their expectations and dreams are not met. Below are the main approaches to help your child resolve the frustration challenges:

❖ **Recognize the emotions of your kids.**

Maybe your son or daughter wasn't cast into the school play or didn't graduate from kindergarten. Maybe he or she wasn't invited for a party or something really serious was the disappointment. Parental response first and foremost is listening and recognizing:

❖ **As a parent, validate your kids.**

The mental distress for children is frustration. Children turn to their parents for guidance as they battle a loss or a failure.

Deception is humiliating, but it is disgraceful. This doesn't make anyone any less. Don't find anything that you like isn't a 'loser.'

This is very necessary, both in words and in actions, to make it clear, because very unfavorable decisions are everywhere. The irony of the community in which we live is that schools and sports are constantly assessed and rated.

The argument that we will all work and aspire to get the belief, that in order to be acknowledged, you have to be a "winner," a "number one." It is unlikely in general, and that was exactly what your kid witnessed. Nasty remarks from the schoolyard will reinforce the feeling of 'loser.' Take a look at public disappointments to discourage bullying.

❖ Walk to your conversation

By learning, children know a lot better than from what you do. Show your children how frustration you are struggling with. Show them how you're coping. You will then be inspired and potentially try to emulate you.

❖ Wish more than getting

Not all deceptions are eternal. Perhaps right now you haven't been able to fly, but next month you'll. Speak to your family. Ask your friends. Discuss how short-term frustration can be accepted and optimism for the future. Seek together to figure out how practical this drive is. This learning tool is particularly useful when the deceit entails not having a desired object, a trip to disneyland, etc. It is a very valuable lifelong skilful experience to discuss our goals and desires, on the one side and what reality can offer at any moment on the other. Now is the time to educate and support your kids.

❖ Children's self-soothing skills.

Many infants learn self-reassuring techniques from an early stage such as walking, chewing pacifiers, and cuddling with their parents. Take note of the kids' self-reassuring skills.

If you're disappointed, suggest you try it. Another way to help them cope with frustration is to draw up a list of qualities they consider to be valuable or ready to learn.

❖ Solutions (without dismissing them).

Most deceptions can be embraced over time, but some can be checked and their results converted. Others can only be acknowledged. Start a brainstorming session to see what ideas you can bring to your child's problem. Be mindful that it's important not to make your child believe you're guilty of failure because they haven't first of all found a solution. Kids can tell! Kids can tell!

If your child is fooled, particularly where the deception is associated with successes, you have a great opportunity to teach them that you love them as they are. Strengthen that they don't meet any conditions to earn your love or to retain it.

Tools to Help Kids Manage Fear and Be Less Anxious

All of our fucks have been stunned lately by bombs, tornadoes, terror warnings, hurricanes, school firefights and major storms, but don't forget our guys. Many parents know what is always characteristic of a disaster or accident whether at home or in the sea—the concerns of their children are growing.

While we all dream of carefree days for our babies, the fact is that our world is unpredictable. Scary things happen. Scary things happen. The children cannot be shielded from unknown events. So we can't "speak out of their fears."

The child's anxiety is real. That works is offering the kid "resources" to handle his worries and concerns.

Best of all, if we encourage our children to use these techniques sufficiently to make their lives routines our children will use them.

The next measures are well-established directions in which you should guide changes — such as modeling courage, watching the media and slowly improving children's resilience — that help children confront their daily concerns in healthy ways and avoid insecurity from shortening existence. As any anxiety-creating situation, each child is special. It is for us to help our children discover the right approach for them as parents, consultors and educators.

1. Teach children to track alarming media use.

Images from movies, video games, music videos, blogs and even TV news can build or intensify fears. Track the television viewing of your child and be especially concerned in whether your child looks closer to bedtime.

Best of all, instruct your kid to use the remote app to uninstall what he knows about it. "It's scary. It's a perfect line for children to know to say, I don't need to watch it.

Help your child always know what it takes to watch both soothing and scary: comedies! Have many DVDs ready for children to pop into as anxieties rise. Make them ready for them. It lets our children learn to track their own diets in the media.

2. As a family, express thoughts.

Encourage you to think about your child's concerns. Having a question in writing makes it much easier to deal with. The aim is to catch her issues early before they go out of proportion and make sure she knows you are going to listen. Then you will comfort your child and explain misunderstandings and answer questions.

Ask your family about your emotions as well, if you're thinking about your problems, children know that it's "Safe" to speak up.

3. Grant cool assistance.

Help your child feel safe and happy. And don't lose your words' power. "You will be all right" (or get the same assurance from daddy holding her hand) will make you feel better to be confident to deploying in certain tough times, as your child experiences anxiety and feels your warmth. Your help words should be a guide that your child will use. Our children mirror our thoughts as we cope. Then show how you should deal with your own problems that your kid needs to imitate. Hold yourself strong, too. Children's fears are captured or spread. Take a look, particularly after or during a trauma, at your doubts or pessimisms.

4. Help your kid know what he's doing.

Many worries we can't shield our children and we just have to face them. And it will remove misperceptions and improve protection if you teach your child about the situation.

Share the school safety program if, for example, your child is worried about school health. Also let him be informed of the emergency preparation of the principal and staff. Indicate so the entire city mayor, cops, a fire service, doctors know what to do in an emergency. Place the keys at school doors that can be accessed at "lockdown"

During the presentation, be cool and honest. First of all, maybe you would like to know, "Would you like to explore what your school is doing to keep you safe? "To remind your kid that there is a Program (after you search to make sure one is posted) visit your child's website.

5. Please read books on anxiety.

Speaking songs, conducting scenarios or reading books about a common terrifying situation may help children con□uer fears. The technique is referred to as "Bibliotherapy" or book recovery. This is helpful as children also remember the character who expresses the same anxiety: "Oh yeah! Another human thinks the same thing!

"Children will reveal their questions to you most likely. Fear will also help to alleviate child anxiety by bringing fear into words.

6. Claim self-declarations minimizing anxiety.

Teach your child to be scared by training it to utter a meaningful sentence. It is best to help your child choose only one sentence and repeat it many times a day, so she can express herself when she is worried. It's best to support your child "I can do this." "I'll be fine." "This isn't a big deal." I can live with it."

7. Exercise methods of relaxation.

If your child is stressed because of anxiety, practicing coping techniques will aid. You will have to place an picture memory on the fridge or next to bed with your baby. Repeat the same tip over and over until it is almost automatic. Your kid is the trick because the worry comes before he works up to use that tactic.

Loving Ways To Raise Resilient Kids

Families are also advised that frustration is healthy for babies, because the world is filled with anger as they grow up. It's like saying it's a dark and cruel world where your child has to learn to sleep without any blankets.

What we really want is to raise children with the ability to find or to make blankets (and to create a healthier environment in which everybody will find blankets!).

The belief that loss creates durability has become prevalent. However, when they lose and do not have the encouragement to try again and again, all that they know is that they are losers. Deception or loss is just half the picture. Resilience doesn't come from loss, but from trying to pick yourself up, try to survive even though something goes wrong. At least this needs some positive practice and a lot of moral support.

It is true, however, that we all learn from challenges, but we still learn the most when we excel, and this motivates us to tackle more challenging challenges. Loss without assistance produces a process of mistrust, defeat and further loss. On the other side, Dominance gives rise to supremacy.

1. Stop controlling and begin coaching.

Coaches help children develop skills; however children are playing the game. Your job as a parent is to help your child grow and succeed. Doing something for them offers a kid a chance to become professional. Doing stuff for them reveals how to create faith and confidence. It ensures that we have to deal with our own anxiety to unlock our energy needs.

2. Recall that the target is not excellence.

Avoid the tentation to "transform" the role of your infant, unless the outcome is critical. Behavior destroys the confidence of a infant.

3. Let them learn to do it from a young age.

Rest in fear on your own. That is not to give them up. Stay here laughing and ready to assist your child in any way, just stay a little behind and hold your hands to yourself, unless you really need encouragement.

You are worrying how much you are concerned about scaling the tower, so it may make you feel better, so it will show your concern on other parents on the playground, but it will not benefit your boy. Currently, it inhibits them.

Just check whether you are safe and then look about to find them. Proudly smile. Smile. Tell, "See! I see that you will do that!" (Which, after all, is what inspired the people to do it?)

4. When they slip, you would be able to catch them. Help them create confidence through the obstacles they face.

This "scaffolding" may be described as the foundation on which your child is developed by emotional development researchers. You demonstrate how to do it, you recommend a plan with words or you just see something.

This helps them to excel as they do something new, and with your guidance they find no experience in doing new ideas themselves. Scaffolding also tells children that nonjudicial help is still available if necessary. Before you reach puberty, you want your children to have such a faith in their bones.

5. Don't program them for failure.

Provide framework for performance. When you see weakness in the future or "will they learn a lesson," will you move in?? A tough decision still. Children should be saved from critical lectures. However, children will interpret that as not being accepted when they see their parents stand by their faces and struggle.

Rather of playing the clarinet or reading the instruction in the science package, they get the impression that they are failures, are unable to handle themselves and their parents have not been cautious enough not to make them struggle or encourage them to control themselves.

Yet doesn't it "rescue" them?

This just depends on how it works. When you take over the science fair and do the half the evening before it is set, that's not rescue; your kid doesn't even know you can save them if he goes out.

However, if you help arrange your plans and work through any step of the way and fight the temptation of changing the project, it completes the task, incredibly proud and learnt about preparing and executing a complicated project.

6. Supporting and educating self-encouragement.

All people deserve to be motivated. This not only serves to inspire and motivate the kids, but it also gives them an inner voice to support themselves for the remainder of their lives. They also encourage their children.

Evidence suggests that it is better for children to learn challenging challenges and communicate in tough circumstances. Give your kid maxims as it becomes tough to repeat them as mantras. 'Practice is making progress!' and 'Do it again, if you are not successful!' and 'I hope I can, I know I can!' have been designed to help us control our disappointment.

If you have to have a piece on the piano or hit the bases full, you need an automated, confident internal voice to inspire and empower them. The stern speech criticizers would otherwise move in, induced by the deceit.

7. Describe and empathize instead of judging.

Praise assesses the result of the behaviour of the infant: "Great work!" It doesn't give the kid any insight about what was great or why you felt it was good. They are encouraged to focus on external sources to determine their jobs.

Through allowing them the ability to judge for themselves, you will boost your support and represent your child more efficiently. Simply explain what they did and felt like: "You've just started training and didn't give up... You have to felt so proud that you completed it!"

8. Concentrate on commitment rather than performance.

Give constructive reviews on other issues, such as hard work or perseverance, they have little power over rather than issues, such as being intellectual. This never happens – at 6 or 16 years of age, you do not want them to sit on their laurels. Your goal is for you to test, train, develop and know so you can accomplish goals when you do a lot of effort.

9. Positive self-discussion pattern.

No matter what you model, you'll learn and imitate your brother. Good speaking boosts our mood, which all of us naturally make unlike self-disparaging remarks.

When your child's or yourself's something similarly unpleasant threatens to spill out of your lips, muffle your words.

Most parents know better than telling their child "What an fool!' (and most parents should stop), but too many people do nothing wrong in front of their children in that way. Only don't prepare yourself. (Surely, neither is it healthy for you. Will you let someone else talk of you in this way?)

10. Don't be afraid of the feelings of your kids.

Recall that your sensitivity can be a crucial factor in overcoming your child's disappointment. Rather than rushing in to eradicate the root of anger immediately, let it be a broader environment in which you express your sympathy that it is a matter: *"I'm sorry this is so hard..."*

"It really is frustrating when..."

"This is not how you expected that it will come to pass..."

You can weep and sulk all day, but you can grieve for your sincere love. When they are sorry, they will be willing, particularly if you show your faith. The next day, they will try again. It is the development of endurance for babies.

11. Don't set up an extra disappointment for your kids.

Naturally, the child should be able to face ever more challenging challenges as it faces elevated levels of anger and anxiety. However, these tensions are intrinsic in their development and guarantee fullness of existence.

You may not have any benefit of getting your child upset or perceived negatively. In reality they see this as evidence of your carelessness, which is often expressed in your sense of interest, which destroys your durability.

12. Affirm your child's ability to impact the world.

Competence and superiority are about control and are based on the experience of a infant who has an impact on the environment.

Any child would have natural power limits ("I can't stop the storm, and Mommy cannot stop"), but the more chances you have for making a difference in the world, the more you will see yourself as a capable person.

Ultimately, our job as parents is to get out of a position and it starts when our kids are very young. Eventually these children grow up and live without us. The way they live depends, in part, on our own fear and our tendency towards controlling our kids. You know the old saying to give roots and wings to our children? The origins are unqualified passion. Trust is wings. Confidence. Youth who have bigger lives all of them.

Ways to Deal With Your Child's Aggressive Behavior

When you are a mom, your fair share of tantrums, meltdowns and stress outs will certainly be tackled. Emotional management is an skill that all of us continue to develop and some children need more time than others to self-control. Yet how do you know if the offensive or abusive conduct of your child is not only part of your research, but is out of hand? So what can you help with?

At this point, children appear to use their physical agitation simply because they do not have the verbal capacity to articulate themselves. For eg, it may be common to move a peer on the playground. This violence would not usually be named if it were part of a trend.

* ❖ *Stay Calm:-* When a child shows a lot of feelings, and the parents match that with more emotion, the hostility of the child will increase," says Researchers. Rather, try influencing the child's emotional control.

❖ *Should not give in to tangles or acts of provocation.* When your boy, for example, has tannin in the food shop for having a certain grain, don't enter and buy it. This is fun and reinforces inappropriate behaviour.

❖ *Catch the goodness of your kids.* Reward positive behaviour even though the kid does nothing odd. When dinner is simple, say, "I really like what you have been doing at dinner." Treats and awards are not required. All are strong on their own appreciation and support.

❖ *Aid children learn to communicate by identifying their feelings.* It will reinforce what your kid thinks and promote emotional speech rather than overt expression. For instance, "I will tell you that you really are mad right now."

❖ *Know the habits of your child and identify stimuli.* Will tantrums arise before school every morning? Focus on the morning practice structuring. Divide activities into easy steps and offer reminders such as "We leave in 10 minutes." Set targets, such as time-saving for four out of 5 school days. So recompense your child if it fulfills those objectives.

❖ *Find appropriate opportunities.* Do not concentrate on content or financial goals. Instead, consider thanking your mum or brother, pick what family eats for dinner, or choosing the family's movie night watches.

If your child struggles with self-discipline, it will help you deal with these techniques in your childhood. If the problem seems unmanageable, keep in mind you are not the only one who is battling the actions of your child. Studies can help to address social and behavioural problems for children and families. Tell the names of the experts in your field for your paediatrician.

Ways to Help Kids Think Positive

It is important for children to consider the impact of their feelings, words, acts (and reactions) in order to lay the groundwork for their future welfare. When young children learn to think positively, they are far more likely to live a happy, safe and successful life than adults.

There are many successful ways to guide kids on the better way of life, but in their lives it is up to them, the parents, to move in the best possible direction. Here are few excellent ideas for parents to help you do this.

1. Be a big roll.

It is important to be an outstanding role model if you want children to think positive. Being mindful of your feelings when you have a kid is a straightforward objective when you find that your attitude, your chat and your actions are imitated by others.

Look at your experiences from a positive viewpoint and explain why your choice is significant. Adults know that not all the universe is sun and rainbows, but children at their age can lack that knowledge. With success and loss, they will benefit from it.

2. Support the relaxed feeling of their emotions.

The old idea that "boys do not weep and girls should still be pale" will hinder a child's imagination and desire to take advantage of its own source of affection. It has also been shown that fostering emotional well-being in children, along with many other health and social effects, prevents mental illness later in life.

Know how your child will scream, weep and show its happiness, and that this is all right. Let them live in an atmosphere in which they feel free enough to share what they feel and what they desire in their lives.

3. Teach them the Law of attraction

The attraction law basically means that you now have a chance, in some way, to do what is in line with your most powerful ideas. Kids will learn to concentrate on everything from toilet ty to being leaders once they grasp this idea. Teach the kids to learn properly, as they now are. Know that they are kind to others and caring. If your kid makes a healthy habit, nothing will deter your child from achieving excellence.

4. Be a motivator.

Make the child believe it will be the best. Encourage you to follow your dreams and believe you will do amazing things in your lives.

And if your child struggles, inspire them to get up and start, remind them that there is still a silver coating in any outcome. Recognize their emotions when the child hopes to take first place at the scientific trade fair, but did not. Tell us how to inspire them for the next step. The cool stuff! The only thing you will do occasionally is say you have done your best, look ahead, knowing hope you will get another chance.

5. Teach them how to concentrate on solution

Problem solving is a vital capacity where all children must acquire confidence, think optimistic, and success in their lives. Support them to understand what caused the problem and how they should go past the problem and work on a solution.

Going as soon as possible into the "solution field" would allow them to constantly be positive and be assured that solutions will always be there.

6. Give them freedom to do what they love

Kids need opportunity to do what they want in order to thrive in their own special way. Direct kids to their love and intent safely. Create an atmosphere for learning about what stimulates your life. All has a lesson, and it's up to us to teach that lesson to improve the learning of a child.

7. They should be surrounded by good people

Surround children in an atmosphere that is encouraging, uplifting. Explain to you that you are a member of the people you spend more time with and seek to relate to those who always find that they are good. They will move on in making people feel better from this fertile optimistic climate.

8. Encourage strong morals and values

Kids will be good, positive leaders if positive social values and fundamental beliefs are developed at an early age. The main values of being constructive are to realize what is "right and wrong" when engaging with peers, to make them accountable for their actions and to teach them to carry out obligations. Speak about your own life events, such as returning someone's wallet or making friends at school with a new child, to make them understand well.

9. Ask them about the positive events of their day.

Rather of worrying how their day went, remind them about the good things of their day. Such particular problems allow them to concentrate rather than frustration on their accomplishments. Children who stay focused on constructive thoughts can just carry on through positive experiences.

10. Creates a rich literation.

Encourage reading from a young age. It takes you to places where you can take on your own powers. The ability to strategize and fix challenges enriches a kid who always writes. Give them tickets for libraries, give them puzzles, play bingo, replay and games, and add books. Also programs like Reading Kingdom encourage you to play online as you read.

Ways to Help Your Children Make and Keep Great Friends

Friendship – this intimate friendship with someone else that offers us the chance to feel valued and taken care of – is important at all stages in life. As one of our fundamental needs as human beings the need for love and possessions has long been created. And good, stable relationships have been well established to boost our self-esteem and general well-being. Nevertheless, as important as these relationships are, they are not always simple or normal, particularly for young people.

We also met the outgoing, young youth who is mates with all and services and gracefully handles social circumstances. We also met the poor, nervous youth, who fail to communicate with others and retreat from each colliding and marking friendship. It is just as important to note that, while others have to do with temperament and maturity, as so many facets of teenage growth, having friends is a ability that can be acquired.

You're correct because it appears that when your child was young it was harder for your child to make friends. When children are young, they tend to cultivate and maintain much of their friendships. Parents create "play days," plan events and resolve the new disputes. Families also schedule birthdays, visitors and RSVPs, and ensure sure everybody is included in the kit.

When children grow up they start evolving and forming friendships. Much as so many things about middle schools make teenagers more confident and choosing for themselves, it makes sense that in handling their partnerships they are more autonomous. Some children come effortlessly with the change, while others struggle hard to make friends.

Such struggles for friendship will contribute in a critical period in their growth to a loss of trust and a feeling of disconnection and weakness.

The positive thing is that mates can only master a handful of skills. And as for any new skill, friendship requires self-awareness, direction and practice. Below are few tips to develop social skills of your teenager:

1. Invite your teen to do some reflecting.

Ask them, "What are the characteristics why people want to be the friend? "And above all, 'What do you feel for yourself?' How do you make people know what you want, what you actually want, and who are you? "Instead of only searching for someone with similar values, it makes it obvious to teens who they are and what they respect to make friends who suit them well.

2. Note that your teen doesn't make every recognized adult a BFF.

Teenagers who fail to make friends prefer to give positive emphasis to the first person. You may reveal too much personal details too soon, so if your best friend has other friends, you may get insecure so confused. Let your teen navigate the distinction between a peer versus a person who genuinely knows versus respects you. You'll have to speak with a peer.

3. Teach the teen how to talk to them.

Small speech is a ability which has been learned. For everyone, it's not convenient. For teens that are more introverted, it is particularly challenging. Exercise in light-hearted, informal discussions about simple topics like music, daily school events or assignments. Help them learn how to be optimistic and foster listening , rather than shouting.

4. Let the teenage girls realize the tension is a common aspect.

Only the strongest of friends will clash, but all disagreement does not mean the end of a relationship. Help them learn to fight justice and to know when to sever an point and to refresh them. Especially when it comes to social media where misunderstandings and disagreements are normal and can easily be resolved, remind your teen how important it is to say, "I guess we are both both upset. Tomorrow in person let's think about it. "

5. Live your own thoughts and judgements.

When you don't like the latest friend of your teen and you think your motives are legitimate, ask how to raise them. Startening a conversation with her might well be much better than the more obvious: "Tell me what you think about hanging out with her." "I don't like her! She was a brat! She is a brat! "You should make careful to make clear about the things you don't like if you find like you have to criticise your teens' mate. For instance: "I found that at the last minute she cancels a lot of plans with you," opens a much better talk than "I don't like her. She is arrogant and over greedy! "The teen appreciates the opinion even more than ever, and, if you feel it's been poorly received by a friend, speak up by all means. Be sure you say so in a way that is hopefully understood.

6. Help your teen foster other relationships.

The desire for ties and affiliations goes to partnerships with colleagues. Ensure you and other people feel connected with their lives. When young people have strong and stable relationships that they can rely on endlessly, the roller ride of teenage friendships is much harder to bear.

Friendships can be critical and rewarding throughout the teen years. Depending on others, revealing secrets and letting them get loose makes life easier at any age. Recall that if your teen has trouble with connections, this is not a lost cause. Make sure that the relationship with them is solid and bring them to the knowledge they need to find friends that are good enough for them.

How to Stop Yelling at Your Kids

That impression is familiar to most mothers. The last straw was just pulled by your brother, and you feel swift rage and wrath. You're really close to let this beast scream out. Why do we balance anger and keep our children from raising their voices? Here are the tips to avoid yelling at your children right before you start.

Each mother can feel exhausted, frustrated and angry. Yet how do we keep those emotions from consuming and affecting the entire mood of the people around us? When do we stop upsetting everyone we love? You should look at ten suggestions that you can use to stop the yells before it goes out if you have ever felt guilty of yelling at your children.

1. Be proactive

It's time to clear your plate for the day if you sense like frustration is coming. Of example, that's not always possible, but you should miss at least a few items to prevent additional burden on your plan. Use the remainder of the day to take it easy. Taking this step until you hit the point of boiling.

2. Breathe

Breathing is great! When your pulse is fluttering, shut your eyes and relax. At least five occasions respire profoundly and steadily. This growing feeling would be impaired if you open your eyes.

3. Sing!

It doesn't matter whether you're able to keep a melody or not. You don't challenge the distinction. You're a great mum. Sing away your anger; add it to the mix while you dance your song.

Do you say you're strange, Afraid your children? Super! Super! They'll halt in their tracks and in astonishment they'll stare at you. You might also join, and it should make the mood better. There isn't any better treatment sometimes than a song of Hakuna Matata.

4. Take five.

Five minutes stepping away puts you out of the situation and gives you space to ease the stress. Naturally, that's not always necessary. It is not necessarily a good moment for your kid to see whether the dinner plates flies as well as the frisbees. But take a few minutes before responding if possible to cool down.

5. Update.

Cold water hit your nose. It sounds easy, but it does work. Do not your mascara want to ruin? The next tip can be what you need. No problem.

6. Block

A very successful way to prevent words from coming out later is to use a water mouthpiece. The secret is here: don't drink it until you're cool.

7. Reminisce.

Remember when you were a new-born child. You have counted these little toes and thumbs; you have kissed the rosy feet. You have stroked her little head beneath your fingers, which looks like the mildest silk. You held her on your lap while she snoozed and breathed the sweet new-born scent.

She was free, you were so thankful. She is yours, you are always grateful. Think of how this new little one feels to be relying upon you. It was up to you to feed, improve, and grow it. It was up to you to quiet her tears, massage her back to soothe her. For all this and more, she still counts on you. Know, even though she is not that small, how it feels like having this little boy in your arms and holds him again.

8. Imagine

Imagine how you feel when your kid is shouted. Imagine in his shoes for yourself. Perhaps he had a bad day? Perhaps something else you're not sure of is happening? Speak to him and try from his point of view to see the case. Ask him questions, and just be there for him, if he won't respond. Finally, he will continue to believe you after he has begun to look at you as a human who can understand without sacrificing the value of his feelings.

Kids do suffer from tough issues and it doesn't make them less important, or more successful, if it seems tiny to us adult. Let them feel like you do, and you will all feel better.

9. Bond

Create your children's solid bond. Know, it's not a burden, it's a gift. They're real men, they build a true story. Be your mate, your guide and your trustee. Create experiences of you that you can remember of love. And if you don't feel camera primed, catch these memories. What from their upbringing do you want them to remember? A mum screaming? I doubt that. I doubt it. I know that I do not. I know I do not.

10. Be an example

We all know, and not what we think, that children do as we do. Show them how to grow your children into people who can healthily manage their grievances. When you're upset or disappointed, shouting at them can just teach them to do the same. Know by demonstration to them.

You might not always have a convenient glass of water or you may stop for 5 minutes. So if you have a couple of these choices, you can battle your own angry self.

"But before I yell, my child won't listen," you might say. Many mothers struggle with this, I know how you feel. I do. For suggestions about how to touch your kid without yelling. If you think you could have a kid with a good will.

The next time you get the awful sensation comes, even if your child doesn't even want to cover his ears with words on his hands, "Stop shouting at me! "Try one or more of the suggestions and learn to avoid screaming at your children. Take one of these moves to get you in the middle so your children will learn how to deal with anger in the right way.

So what if you couldn't hold your kid back and shout? Nobody's fine, we're all wrong. Yet what makes you a perfect mother is trying to be different.

Helping a Child Deal With Uncomfortable Emotions

Mentally healthy children recognize that they should control their feelings rather than manipulate them. Children who know how to handle their emotions will regulate their actions and ignore bad ideas. Yet infants are not raised with an awareness of their desires and they are not socially mature naturally when sharing their feelings.

A kid who does not know how to handle his frustration may be violent and sometimes frustrated. Likewise, a kid who has what to do when he is upset will waste hours pouting alone.

If kids don't grasp their feelings, they also can stop something that sounds uncomfortable. An example is the lack of faith in a child who is very uncomfortable in social settings because he is unable to handle the anxiety involved with doing new activities.

Teaching children to control their feelings will every several issues with their behaviour. A girl who knows her feelings would therefore be well prepared and more able to work at its best to cope with uncomfortable circumstances. With instruction and practice, children can learn how to deal healthily with their emotions.

❖ **Teach moral accountability.**

While it is safe for children to have a wide variety of emotions, it is also important to understand that they control their feelings. A child who has had a hard day at school can choose after-school activities which improve his mood. Even a child who is upset about everything that her brother has done will find ways to cope.

Tell your kid the emotional stress will not be an reason for misbehavior. Show them the feeling. Feeling furious does not grant her the right to hurt someone and thoughts of grief do not stop for hours.

Teach your child that he is responsible for his own actions, so to punish someone for his emotions is not appropriate. You should fix her terminics if your kid attacks her sibling and appears to have made her insane. Explain that everyone is responsible for their own thoughts and actions. While her brother may have affected her behavior, he did little to make her feel.

This is as important to note that your child is not responsible for the feelings of other people. When she wants to be safe and anyone else gets offended, that's okay. Kids need to be encouraged in their life so that they can overcome social manipulation to judge for themselves. This is a valuable lesson. Incorporating positive beliefs and healthy character will give your child confidence that, given criticism of some, they are likely to make wise choices.

❖ **Practice Uncomfortable Emotions Tolerating.**

Inconvenient feelings are also expected. When you stand on the cliff's edge, fear is a growing emotional reaction to alert us to danger. However, occasionally we have needless uncertainty and anxiety.

Teach your child that it doesn't automatically mean that it is a bad decision if she feels uncertain about it. For starters, if you're scared to take on football because you're nervous, you won't know any of the other kids, convince them to play anyway.

When it's healthy to do so, voicing her doubts will allow her to see that her is more than she feels.

Kids are often used to avoid frustration and tend to lose self-confidence. You say, "I never could do that, it will be too scary." As such, they lose a lot of life chances.

Move your kid out of the comfort zone gently. Lob her attempts and prove that her desire to try is more important than the outcome. Tell her how to use mistakes as ways to develop her learning and development, loss and awkward circumstances.

❖ How do I help change the bad attitude of a child.

The moods of children frequently rely heavily on outside circumstances. A kid can be happy as she plays and then sad times when it's time to go. And, when she discovers that she will stop by ice cream on her way home, she will easily transform into happiness.

Teach your child that its moods must not be absolutely reliant on outside circumstances. Rather, regardless of the situation, it should have some influence of how it feels.

Give the children more mood-enhancing. It does not actually mean that she will hide or ignore her feelings, but it does mean that she should take action to make her feel happier and that she is not caught in a negative mood. It can just maintain her bad mood, detach herself or lament for hours.

Help your child find the ways that it may create to calm or cheer up when it is upset. Identify those things that can improve her mood. During drawing, one child can benefit from playing outdoors to burn off steam.

Identify different decisions that might be made by your child when it feels bad and motivate them to work and make it feel better. For examples, when you catch her moping, try to say, "I think you could stay steep in a bad mood by moping today. Anything would you do to improve your mood? I wonder? "If you motivate your child to get involved or do something else, your child will control your feelings healthily.

Surprising Reasons Why Kids Misbehave And How to Respond

Children use their actions to explain how they feel and what they think. Sometimes by their actions, they convey what they cannot actually verbalize. Consider the potential root cause of the conduct disorder when deciding what disciplinary technique to use.

1. They ought to be alert.

When parents speak to friends or relatives or are otherwise busy on the phone, children feel lost. And to throw a tanner, yell, or strike a sibling is an outstanding approach. While it's disappointing, kids are always searching for it. Bad behaviour and good behavior commendations were one of the easiest ways to deal with patterns that search for recognition.

2. They're Copying Others

Through watching people, children learn to act. If you see a school peer incorrect or you imitate what they saw on TV, children will replicate it. Limit the children to violent Media, video and real-life behavior. Function a safe example to teach the child to act correctly in various circumstances.

3. They're Testing Limits

They always try to know if you're serious after you've set down rules and asked children what they can't do. We just check boundaries and see what can happen when the rules are violated. Set strong boundaries which consistently have consequences. When children know that they have a slight opportunity, they are always tempted to do it. If you demonstrate that any time they violate a law, they will experience a negative effect, they will begin to follow.

4. Lack of skill

Often issues with actions result from a lack of expertise. A child deficient in social skills may hit a child because he wants to play with a toy. A kid without issues can't tidy the space because his toys don't fit in the tool box, so he's not sure what to do. Instead of actually telling him what to do, when your kid is not behaving properly. Present him harassment solutions so that he can learn from his faults.

5. They want freedom.

When pre-schoolers know more, they also try to explore their learning abilities on their own. Tweens are also known for their equality efforts. They can be more contentious and even rude.

Teens will revolt in an effort to prove that adults will speak for themselves. They could violate the rules deliberately and attempt to show to adults that they don't want to do things.

Give the right choices to your kids. Tell your pre-school children, "You want to drink water or ice cream?" Tell your teenage boy, "There's up to you to determine while you do your internship, so you can use your devices while your research is over!"

6. They can't keep their feelings under control.

Even children don't know what they hear. You can quickly become frustrated, if you're upset, and therefore violent. You will also respond if you are nervous, anxious or bored.

Children must learn to cope with emotions like depression, deceit, anger and fear in a safe way. Teach children about thoughts and teach their children positive ways to control their emotions and prevent misbehaviour.

When children are more able to control their thoughts, they can express their feelings using positive coping strategies. An infant may learn to take time to relax rather than misbehaving to communicate emotions.

7. They Have Unmet Needs

A abuse also occurs when the infant is thirsty, exhausted or sick. Some infants and pre-school students are not successful at when they need to do. We also use their actions to show that we do not meet their needs.

Through watching for unmet needs, parents can help avoid behavioral problems. For starters, take a kid after he's had a nap and snacks are available. Tell your child how he thinks and try evidence that he has unmet needs.

8. They want control and influence.

Power and influence sometimes contribute to misconduct. At times, a child attempts to recover some influence with stubborn and argumentative actions. If a child attempts to manipulate a situation because of behaviour issues, a power struggle may result. One way to prevent a power battle is to give two options to a boy. For instance: "Will you clean your room now or after that TV show is finished? "You can allow children leverage over the situation by giving two options. This can decrease other objections and increase the likelihood that a child complies with instructions 3

9. Misbehaviour works.

One of the most basic causes of misbehaviour by children is that they are hungry. When they violate the rules, they will soon learn that violence works.

For examples, a child whining before his mother comes in discovers that whining is a perfect way for him to get everything he wants. Or a boy who drops a tannin in the middle of a store and his Dad offers to buy him a toy to avoid screaming, points out that the tangle of temper is fine.

Ways To Maintain An Emotional Connection With Your Child

What is emotional protection and why is it important? Emotional health is a term used in the care of people, but it also has a significant effect on children's emotional and psychological well-being. Emotional protection ensures leaders are comfortable enough to become insecure in their partnership. Researchers suggest that people are more likely to be happy in emotionally stable marriages than in emotionally unstable marriages.

An absence of emotional protection can result in an imbalance in neurology and in insufficient social, emotional and communicative behaviour. Studies say that 'attachment' and 'estimation' must be possible before emotional stability can evolve.

Throughout the bond between parent and infant, children may feel emotionally secure because they have a positive connection with their parents and know they are highly valued. The social wellbeing of our children depends primarily on the "vibes" we give them. When they feel protected, children may show their feelings as they know that they are not punished.

1. Love your child

The scientists once said, "You don't have to turn your kids into wonderful people. You just have to consider them as wonderful people. You'll actually believe them if you do that faithfully from the day they are born."

2. Check their feelings.

From inside, mental support arrives. It begins by encouraging your child to connect with various feelings and be confident with them. And in the future, the lack of children's feelings makes life impossible for them. Worse, secondary feelings such as guilt and fear may develop.

Taking note of daily possibilities to help children relate to their feelings. A non-accusatory voice with feelings. When our children are conscious that they have true feelings, they can respond more easily to these feelings.

For eg, if you suggest you appreciate his unbelieving frustration that you don't have the gift he wants, you don't just help him in putting a name to his feelings.

3. Be assured that your personal needs will be met.

An emotionally distant parent leads to a distant emotional boy. Our children can get their feelings and socially stable relationships first and foremost by coping with their own emotions. Our past failures, embarrassment and rage feelings may build concerns that may affect our parenthood. Deal with your own feelings to discourage your child from spreading them unknowingly.

For starters, don't cover up your child's rage, but note that our children are watching us for emotions. Saying "I'm going to take 5 minutes before we chat" tells your child that everyone is upset, but that is an emotion to be handled.

4. Listen first, before responding.

That what lies unspoken there is too much conveyed. Remember that much of the actions of children is emotionally motivated. Listen to the unspoken before you respond. Be careful how you talk when you react. Recall the voice is a strong instrument — your sound is voluminous. To listen carefully to your kid always means to ask questions that allow you to feel comfortable: "Do you want me to come with you?" "How do we improve?" It will help to build the atmosphere in which it feels easy simply to say to your kid, that "I am there."

5. Give yourself more time to communicate and connect.

More opportunity to bond and play will help to build social stability for your child. Interaction encourages safe feelings. Confidence and approval are based on emotionally secure relationships. You make your child a world of success if you prove him that you embrace and enjoy them.

Positive Ways To Help Your Child Learn To Manage Their Anger

Some parents are sending an upset child to their bed to "calm down." Surely when she's angry we can't bargain with her. There is not time to teach or apologise. She must slow down. She must calm down. Why do we yell at our babies, throw our companion into a tangle or overeat in order to avoid noticing our frustration.

Rather, what should we do? We should help our children learn to cope responsibly with their frustration. Most of us find it difficult to imagine what it feels like. Clearly placed, rational control of indignation starts by acknowledging our frustration, but by not harming anyone. In the other party, there is still a way to express what we need.

Once we are prepared to stop, we really found pain and anxiety and tristness because we recognized the underlying feelings of our frustration. When we can sense these feelings, the rage is dissipating. It was just a safety reaction.

It is one of the most important childhood activities — tolerating frequent wounds without emotional fury. Those who can do so will collaborate for others and continue to accomplish their goals. We call them wise mentally. When we tell children that all their emotions are all right, they still have a say about how they behave.

How do I do that here.

1. Move away from "fight or flight"

After taking a few deep breaths and realizing that no emergency occurs. This coaching makes the kid feel better and allows him / her to get out of "fight or flight."2.

2. Pay attention

Recognize why the kid is frustrated. Often people are complaining because they don't feel noticed. In comparison, the kid will continue to feel calmer, even though he doesn't come his way, though it feels understand.

3. Try to see from his viewpoint.

"Oh, Sweetie, sorry it's too tough. You're thinking I cannot understand you....that has to sound terrible and alone." You don't have to accept and you've not got to deny. The more caring you become the more apt your kid becomes to find a path through the emotions and worries in the middle of rage. Recognize only in the moment his reality. His reality will change if he feels understood.

4. Don't get trapped by disrespectful and intimate attacks.

When children scream at them, parents are also upset. However, the kid doesn't hate you or want a new mum or dad or whatever she yells. And she's having the most disturbing thing she can think of, and you'll see how angry she's. She's devastated and scared and helpless. Tell me why you're confused. I'm listening. "Your kid isn't" behaving poorly "or" playing, "she tells you in the best way she can today, exactly how angry she is. You must be too frustrated to mention it to me. When she realizes that she does not have to lift her voice, or that it is safe to show her vulnerable emotions, she will develop the ability to express her feelings better.

5. **Set any boundaries required to safeguard both while acknowledging the rage and sympathy.**

"You're so angry, you should be as crazy as you want to, so punching isn't all right anyway, no matter how frustrated you are. Do not speak, but to convince her that she is healthy. Unless your kid is still in total disintegration. Don't bother teaching, explaining or justifying. It is not time to justify why she can't get what she wants or to make her admit that she really likes her little sister, because she's awash in adrenaline and other fight or flight reactions. The hurricane is your only job now. Only confess, how angry she is: "I'm sorry it's so hard to be sad about it ...."

6. **If your child is already in a full meltdown, don't talk except to empathize and reassure her that she's safe.**

Don't try to teach, reason or explain. When she's awash in adrenaline and other fight or flight reactions is not the time to explain why she can't have what she wants or get her to admit that she actually loves her little sister. Your only job now is to calm the storm. Just acknowledge how upset she is: "You are so upset about this...I'm sorry it's so hard."

7. **Remind yourself that tantrums are nature's way of helping immature brains let off steam.**

The neuronal mechanisms that regulate themselves are not yet in order for infants. The easiest way to help children in maintaining such neuronal networks, when they're angry and at times is to have empathy to them! (and we don't always control our anger well, even as adults!) It's all right, fine, really, that your child shows those enmeshed, furious, hurt feelings. They feel closer to us and more confident after supporting children with a tantrum. They fear less internally so that they can be more compassionate emotionally. They're not as rugged and stiff.

8. Remember that anger is a defense against a threat.

It comes from our answer to "war, fly or freeze." The hazard is outside of us sometimes, but it's generally not. We always see risks outside of us as we bear old packed feelings such as pain, terror or sorrow. So whatever happens at this moment causes these old emotions, and we go to the stage of battle to attempt and bring them down again. (It's not a threat to your health or well-being)

And while your child might be upset at something right now, it may also be that he is trapped in a complete emotional bag that he only wants the old tears and worries to communicate. A fresh suffering will sound like a child ending up in the universe because there are all the same emotions that emerge. Children must do whatever they can to overcome these unpleasant emotions, and they're screaming.

9. Make it safe for your child to move past anger.

When you are confident of voicing your rage, and with kindness we meet this frustration, the rage is starting to melt. So it is not the vengeance that heals as we embrace the vengeance of our husband. It is the sound of tears and fears under the fury, which washes away the wound which tristess, which allows the cold to disappear, because the fury is not sufficient any longer to protect as the child reveals the more insecure emotions.

10. Hold as tight as possible.

Also when he is upset, your child wants a spectator acknowledging who loves him. Once you're waiting for a embrace, I am right here. Unless he calls out "Go away!" say "You want me to go away and I go back again, all right? I'll not leaving you with these terrifying emotions, so I'm going back."

11. Keep yourself safe.

Kids often benefit from pushing against us when they're upset, so if you can tolerate it and stay compassionate, that's fine to allow. But if your child is hitting you, move away. If she pursues you, hold her wrist and say "I don't think I want that angry fist so close to me. I see how angry you are. You can hit the pillow I'm holding, or push against my hands, but no hurting." Kids don't really want to hurt us— it scares them and makes them feel guilty. Most of the time, when we move into compassion and they feel heard, kids stop hitting us and start crying.

12. Do not try to determine whether he responds too strongly.

He's over-reacting, obviously! Yet know that kids get hurt and panic every day they can't verbalize or really understand that we don't. We store them and then try a chance to "discharge." And if your kid is collapsing over the blue cup so you can't even get the blue cup out of the car right now, it's all right that he lovingly embraces his crumble. This wasn't for the cup much of the time, or something he wants. Whether children are whiny and uncomfortable, they typically just have to cry.

13. Recognizing her frustration allows her to calm a bit.

Then help her get under the anger by calming. When you may feel sympathy for this battling young man, she can feel it and return it. Only empathize, don't study. "I'm so sorry, Sweetie." She's going to actually pause and pause reckless, until you know the emotions beneath your rage. Many flaws or even tears are obvious. You will encourage her to uncover those feelings by concentrating on the original trigger:"I am so sad that you can't get the that you love, my friend. I'm sad that this is really hard." And all the frustrated emotions are dissipating.

14. You can chat, If he calm down

Stop the temptation to talk. Say a story to help him contextualize the big surge of feeling. "It was some huge emotions ... everyone has to weep occasionally ... you wanted ... I said no, you were so disappointed ... you were really angry ... you were really sad and disappointed .... thank you for telling me how you felt ...." You should ride back to wind down later in the day or when you snuggle. Yet most young children would like to hear the story, as long as it's a story, not a lesson, about how they got angry and wept. This makes you feel understood and it allows you to understand yourself.

15. What about teaching? You don't have to do as much as you think.

What she did was false, your child knows. Such wonderful feelings made her realize that it was an emergency and that she had to follow the law of being kind. You're less likely to commit an infraction by helping her handle the feelings.

Wait for it and then leave things straight after the emotional conclusion. Identify and coordinate the part of her next time she tries to take a better path. Make sure that she offers her a chance to help solve her question. "If we get too upset, we forget how much we love the other person as well, just when you were really upset at your friend, they seem like they're our enemy, oK? You got so very mad at her, we all get so mad, we feel like we strike, but if we did, then we're sorry we're hurting someone else. Gradually the child is mindful of how unhappy the weather is and that even if it cannot always get what it wants, he will always get better—one who loves him and embraces him and the yucky bits, such as frustration and rage. He should have understood that feelings are not dangerous – by relying on them they can be accepted and passed on. Gradually, without hitting the other guy, he can learn to verbalize his thoughts and desires even though he is angry.

You're trying to show him how to control his feelings. And instead of eroding your link with him, you would have improved. Everyone take a deep breath and in the face of fury remain caring. I mean, it sounds sweet, so you can't get that out all the time. But you can encourage your child to build the neuronal networks for a more emotionally aware brain every time you do. Then you would be much less dramatic — and have more respect for yourself.

Conclusion

The best way of coping with and handling violence is to help children properly communicate their frustration. For a cause, we have these emotions, and the more we continue to hide and cover up the more violence takes on a new shape and finally appears.

You are still able to hear the good phrases without being too harsh at first. It will allow them to comprehend their great angry feelings. Then show them that getting upset doesn't change anything and expressing frustrated feelings just worsens matters. It is necessary to teach them how to verbally name and talk out, rather than act on these emotions.

In certain cases, even voicing frustration increases the likelihood of improving the outcome accordingly. This helps to motivate and support this approach in a constructive way. In short, the infant knows the benefits that frustration is managed and properly articulated.

Children will be encouraged to convey frustration properly as early as possible. Emotions are not accurate until they begin to surface. Emotions are accurate. Younger kids know lessons again and again in rehearsal and repeat. It needs time, so sooner or later it has to be dealt with. It may go much better if you practice your listening right next to your boy.

As a parent with a child with behavioural problems, one of the most valuable things you can do is to learn and provide best possible solutions.

It can be very difficult to control children's frustration because of their unique disposition. This could get worse as they try to hide from their parents their rage. As parents, though, we will be able to learn and know what prompted them to get upset. We should use these tips to help children handle their frustration, to demonstrate their sensitivity and composure when upset, and in serious situations we can seek medical guidance or clinical support. In this way, we should even provide them with assistance when they become angry.

Printed in Great Britain
by Amazon